MANAGING
FOR
PERFORMANCE

MANAGING FOR PERFORMANCE

How to Get the Best Out of Yourself and Your Team

ALASDAIR WHITE

Alasdair White
May 97

PIATKUS

Copyright © 1995 by PMS Limited

First published in 1995 by
Judy Piatkus (Publishers) Ltd of
5 Windmill Street, London W1P 1HF

First paperback edition 1996

The author has asserted his moral rights

'Personal Leadership Profile II' on p. 90 copyright © LPT 1990
'Personal Behaviour Profile' on p. 107 copyright © LPT 1990
All reproduced by permission of Sandy Ellvers-Dix

A catalogue record for this book is
available from the British Library

ISBN 0-7499-1446-7 (hbk)
ISBN 0-7499-1576-5 (pbk)

Typeset by Computerset, Harmondsworth
Printed and bound in Great Britain by
Biddles Ltd, Guildford and King's Lynn

For Fiona, Riba and Siobhan
whose understanding and support
made this book possible

Acknowledgements

It is normal for authors to thank all those who have contributed in any way to the writing of the book. Amongst the many others who have helped and to whom I am indebted, I would like to give special thanks to Philippe Paillart, Tom Evans, Jean-Francois Hautemulle, Karl Sergeant and Bryn Thomas, all of whom provided me with opportunities to develop, refine and test the ideas and skills presented in this book. I would also like to thank Sandy Ellvers-Dix and Lee Bushby of LPT Productions for allowing me to use their questionnaires and the Personal Time Profile on page 44.

Contents

Acknowledgements　　vi
Introduction　　1

Part I　What are we trying to achieve, and how will we achieve it?　　2

1　Management and Performance Management　　5
2　Objectives and Planning　　13

Part II　Who is going to achieve the objective?　　28

3　Personal Development　　31
4　Management Style – the Key to Success　　82
5　People: the Human Resource　　128
6　Team Development – Coaching and Training　　153
7　Motivation　　168

Part III　Achieving the objective　　180

8　Office Environment – Physical and Psychological　　183
9　Cause, Commitment and Goals　　194
10　Feedback – Seeing how we are doing　　212
11　Where Do You Go From Here?　　230

Select Reading List　　232
Index　　238

Introduction

I have always found managing people a fascinating, frustrating, exhilarating, and extremely satisfying experience. The purpose of this book is to provide you with a range of techniques and ideas to make your management experience more rewarding, to help you achieve your objectives, and to help you **manage for performance.**

I was persuaded to write this book by the many managers who have come on my Performance Management Workshop seminar over the last three years. At the beginning of the week there was often a healthy degree of scepticism about the ideas presented – "after all, wasn't this just another managing people type seminar" – but by the end there was commitment.

This commitment was carried out into the workplace with outstanding results. One business actually achieved a 50 per cent growth in profits following the implementation of all the concepts outlined and they clearly believed that the workshop's training and ideas were what made it happen. Similar results have been achieved elsewhere – but I would like to make a very important point: **the techniques and skills outlined in this book are only that – techniques and skills; it requires YOU to put them into practice and to make them work**. Putting them into practice takes time and commitment and you must not expect an instant improvement in performance from your team – give it time and keep going even when the going is hard.

Each chapter follows the same basic, easy-to-understand, structure – first there is a discussion of the theory and techniques involved, then we look at how to apply them and finally there is a brief bullet-point summary of the basic points.

Part I
What are we trying to achieve, and how will we achieve it?

1
Management and Performance Management

What is a manager? • what is 'Performance Management'? • what makes people 'tick'? – the theory of motivation • different management styles for different people • office environment – a help or a hindrance?

WHAT IS A MANAGER?

WHAT IS a manager? There are, of course, hundreds of answers to that question. My starting point is to define a manager as someone who *manages* a process and *leads* a team of people. If you have anybody reporting directly, or indirectly, to you then you are a manager and your main responsibility is to manage their activities and lead them towards delivering a superior performance. And to do this you need to use a range of people-management techniques – you need to be a leader.

But what is a leader? I do not see the role of a leader as being different from that of a manager – it is part of the same thing – and I generally use the two words interchangeably. However, if you visit any large book shop and look at the titles on the shelves in the business section, you will find that many books, perhaps hundreds, have been written on the subject of leadership – what makes a good leader, and what are the qualities of a leader. Unfortunately for the general reader, much of the analysis has been undertaken by, and many of the books written by, academics, who mystify rather than demystify the subject. Almost all the material suggests that leaders are born, not made, and that you cannot learn to be a leader.

This is not true.

Professor John Adair, when studying leadership, concluded that the most practical way to examine leadership was to observe what a leader does. Whilst acknowledging that leadership qualities and the situation in which the leader works undoubtedly play a part, Adair believes these aspects do not go far enough in determining success, and it is the actions that leaders need to take that are the most important. He narrowed these down into three critical areas:

- achieving the task
- building the team
- developing the individual.

Adair concludes that it is the balance between these three areas that determines the success of the leader, and that if they are out of balance for any length of time there are likely to be adverse consequences.

I believe we can use the Adair model to look at the role of the manager – especially since the modern manager needs to be a leader. I think it is reasonably clear to most of us that the prospects for the old-style manager who was nothing but a glorified supervisor are strictly limited – much more is expected of today's manager as companies de-layer, restructure, and re-engineer to allow them to succeed in the 1990s. The manager of today *has* to be a leader.

There are three clear areas of responsibility that all managers have to accept:

- the responsibility for determining how the objective of the team will be achieved
- the responsibility for ensuring the team members are selected, developed, trained, and carry out their responsi-

bilities to a pre-determined standard that will allow them to achieve their objective, and

- the responsibility for the motivation, performance, and personal development of the individual team members so that the objective is achieved.

The first area of responsibility is one of planning ('achieving the task'), the second is one of team building and training ('building the team'), and the third is one of performance management ('developing the individual'). Unfortunately, most managers fail to plan – instead, they fight fires – they accept the team they are given and do little to develop it, and they have little understanding of performance management. The result is that they fail to achieve their objectives and generally blame 'the bosses' for unrealistic goals. In many companies this sort of management behaviour goes unchallenged due to a corporate culture that only pays lip service to accountability and extracts no retribution for failure.

To be effective managers we have to ensure that we are effective in each of the main areas, to understand that they are interdependent, and to keep them in balance. The key is the ability to manage **people**: the skills involved in getting them to deliver their best performance are ones which we can all develop. It is a matter of learning to use a range of techniques in an appropriate manner: techniques we can all learn, which are not difficult to apply, and which are based on common sense and an understanding of why people do things.

WHAT IS 'PERFORMANCE MANAGEMENT'?

Performance Management is applying these techniques to get the best possible performance from you and your team in any given circumstance, so that you can achieve your goals and objectives. This is a very sweeping statement, so let me explain.

Let me start by defining 'performance'. The *Oxford English Dictionary* defines 'performance' as 'the process or manner of performing' or 'to accomplish or to execute'. Therefore, the best performance is 'the best process of accomplishing' whatever it is you want to accomplish – be it reaching a sales goal, making a profit, getting more out of your life, winning a medal, becoming a concert pianist or anything else you care to mention.

Secondly, the *OED* defines 'to manage' as 'to have under effective control', with 'management' being the 'process of managing'.

Given these definitions, it is clear that 'Performance Management' is the effective control of the best process of accomplishing whatever has to be accomplished.

A great deal has already been written about almost all aspects of management and many influential thinkers have turned the whole subject into a 'science', with rules, processes, theories, and all the paraphernalia that entails. We have scientific management, situational management, behavioural management, and many more schools of thought, all of which have valid contributions to make to understanding the role of the manager within organizations, **but fail to address themselves to the enhancement of the performance of the individuals who make up that organization and on whom its success depends.**

In Performance Management we are not concerned with the business systems and processes that are involved in our work, nor are we deeply concerned with scientific management theories – although a little background is called for to explain why the techniques work. What we are concerned with is the management of people and how you can obtain a better performance from yourself and your team. To be an effective Performance Manager you have to manage your own performance effectively if you are to manage the performance of others.

How do you do this? The starting point must be to know what you and your team have to achieve and by when – this establishes the **goal**. The next step is to develop an overall **plan** outlining how you are going to achieve your goal. This plan will then define what **resources** you are going to need – especially the human resources.

You must then acquire those resources, select and recruit the necessary people, develop and train them, and then manage their performance. And don't forget, **you** are one of your resources and you will need to look at *your* management styles, *your* skills, *your* strengths and weaknesses, as well as those of your people. In the following chapters, we will be looking at these issues in depth and I will be offering help and guidance on how to find the necessary people and how to develop them and yourself, so as to achieve your objectives.

Beyond this, there are three main requirements for the successful management of people:

- to understand what makes a person 'tick' – why they work and for what reason: their motiviation for doing things
- to understand the need for different management styles in different circumstances, and
- to understand the impact of the environment on the ability of a person to deliver an optimum performance.

Let's take a brief look at the background to each of these.

What makes people 'tick'? The theory of motivation

Back in the early 1960s thinkers in the USA were attempting to develop a theory of 'why people do things' – a grand theory of life, so to speak. The result was encapsulated as: 'people only do something if they obtain a psychological or material benefit from doing it'.

In other words, people act only for selfish reasons. This is hard to fault – the main argument against it being that people sometimes act for altruistic reasons, to which the theory's supporters answer: apparently altruistic actions supply a psychological and emotional 'gain' or benefit to the person taking the actions.

Motivation has an unhealthy stablemate, **manipulation**. Motivation can be defined as 'getting people to do what *they* want', whereas manipulation is 'getting people to do what *we* want'. Clearly, if people do things only to obtain a benefit for themselves then they will certainly be motivated to do what *they* want – equally, it is sometimes hard to see how doing what *we* want them to do will provide them with a benefit.

So, the first key to successful motivation is to get your people to really want what they want – because in seeking to achieve what they want, they will deliver an optimum performance. The more they desire to do what they want, the greater their performance. The management skill is to succeed in persuading your people **to want what *you* want** because in this way your objectives and those of your team become the same and they will be motivated to achieve – this process is centred around goals and goal-setting. In terms of corporate management, your objectives, as a manager, should be those of the organization itself.

The second key to success is to maintain the motivation of your people – this is rather more difficult to achieve and is the area in which most managers fail. They believe that once they have motivated their people that is all there is to it – but they are wrong: once motivation is established it never lasts and has to be constantly re-established – a process which is based on performance monitoring and feedback.

Chapter 7 covers the subject of motivation – what it is, and what it is not – and will try to establish some simple rules.

DIFFERENT MANAGEMENT STYLES FOR DIFFERENT PEOPLE

Steve Jones was a manager who took pride in being a 'straight-talking' man and he had led his sales team in the successful development of new markets and the launch of new products. The job had required a forceful, hands-on approach to getting things done and his team appreciated Steve's straight-talking leadership – they knew where they stood and knew they could rely on him to help them achieve their goals. Steve was a successful Performance Manager.

After his department had done all that was asked of them, and more, Steve was asked to become a main Board director, in charge of sales and marketing and with a brief to 'drive the sales up'. However, within months he was faced with hostility from his fellow directors, a deteriorating performance amongst the sales team, and demoralisation in the marketing department. After a year, the sales performance was no better and the Board was considering calling for his resignation.

Fortunately, the Chairman saw what the problem was and intervened.

He took Steve aside and together they analysed the situation. It soon became clear that the main issue was Steve's style of management – his straight talking was perceived as aggressive and abrasive by his fellow directors; his forceful, hands-on approach was perceived as interference by the creative team in the marketing department; and the sales team now saw him as trying to rule by diktat. All in all, Steve's earlier successful management style was no longer appropriate in his new role and he had failed to change his approach.

What the Chairman knew, and Steve had found out, is that different people and different circumstances require different management styles – what is a successful style in one circumstance is often inappropriate in another.

In Chapter 3 we look at how you yourself can develop as a manager, while Chapter 4 examines the whole subject of management style in greater detail. I have included some questionnaires to help you understand your own style.

OFFICE ENVIRONMENT – A HELP OR A HINDRANCE?

We all know that being in a cold office can stop us working at our best – and, equally, an office that is too hot has the same effect. Similarly, the amount of light available, the availability of proper equipment, and the quality of the air all have an impact on our performance.

Our non-work work environment can also have a major impact – the cleanliness of the toilets, the availability of refreshments, and the colour scheme are just three areas of environmental impact. In fact, it is the quality of these things that tell a visitor more about the company than all the literature available. Consider for a moment: you walk into a top restaurant and you know the bill is going to be high, but you are looking forward to the meal; you decide to visit the toilet before ordering and find it is less than clean – how does your perception of the restaurant change? If you are like most people, you will feel a lot less happy about the food, the service, and the bill – you may even choose to leave the restaurant.

Many people unconsciously form opinions about the management of a company based on environmental things – and this is often expressed as, 'If they don't care about the conditions in which we have to work, how can they really care about us?' If your people believe you do not care about them, then you have little chance of their delivering a good performance.

Environmental issues go beyond the physical conditions in which we have to work: the attitude of the team members to each other, the 'political' environment within the company, and the 'market' environment in which we work, also affect our ability to deliver an optimum performance. These subjects are important and we will see how improved communication can overcome some of the downside.

SUMMARY POINTS

- As the manager, you must take responsibility for planning how the team objectives are to be achieved, for building the team, and for developing and motivating the individual members.
- The key to leadership is managing people so they deliver their best performance in any given circumstance.
- Performance Management is the application of the management techniques necessary to achieve superior performance.
- To obtain a top performance from your people you must understand what makes them 'tick' – what motivates them.
- People are motivated by what *they* want to achieve: as their manager, you have to make what *they* want and what *you* want as close as possible.
- Motivation, once established, never lasts – you must continually reinforce the motivation of your team by monitoring and feedback.
- You have to understand that different people and different situations require different management styles – you must use the most appropriate management style.
- You must take into account the environment in which you operate – your people (and you) are affected by your environment which can help or hinder performance.

2
Objectives and Planning

Define the objectives • define the resources and constraints • capacity planning – the vital exercise • a Sales Capacity Planning Exercise • what happens when goals and performance are incompatible? • plan your work • the Action Plan • work your plan

IN MOST CORPORATIONS, sometime in the third quarter, a meeting takes place to decide on the goals and objectives for the following year. This meeting, generally called the annual budget meeting, attempts to define what the business has to achieve to meet the requirements of the Five Year Plan, or whatever measure of success the company uses. Normally, only senior management are involved and the meeting focuses on reviewing the current performance against plan, forecasting the likely outcome of the year's activities, and – based on this – what could reasonably be achieved the following year in terms of turnover, revenue, and profits. The leading figure in many of these meetings is the finance director – he is the one with all the numbers, he generally controls the forecasting, and he is the one who will have produced the report from which everyone will work.

If senior management has a good understanding of the business and the market in which it operates, the numbers in the finance director's report should be reasonably accurate, allowing the management team to discuss the strategic objectives. Such a discussion will focus on 'what we want to achieve', what markets the business is to operate in, and what products or services have to be provided to deliver the levels of profits desired. A good strategic discussion should result in a good strategic plan – one that can be broken down into its component parts and handed over to more junior managers to be turned into tactical action plans.

Unfortunately, in many companies, the annual budget meeting turns into a turf war with each of the principal managers defending the performance of their department and focusing on the tactical issue of 'how we are going to achieve the numbers' rather than a strategic discussion about 'what we want to achieve'. The goals that come out of such a meeting are then handed down and unquestioningly accepted by managers all down the line until they reach the level of the manager who actually has to deliver the performance. At this point the goals are likely to be greeted with disbelief, derision, and frustration – but they are just numbers and there is little point in trying to appeal. In a huge number of cases, the result is that the goals are not met, the objectives are not achieved, and no one has to take the blame – the manager collects his annual increase, his staff continue as normal, and a generally low level of motivation pervades the organisation. The attitude in the minds of the managers is: 'If goals don't have to be achieved, then why try to achieve them?'

So who is to blame for this sorry situation? Senior management for not being strategically orientated? Middle managers for not questioning the goals? Or the manager who accepts the goal with little hope of achieving it?

Initially, the blame rests with senior management. Most people feel more comfortable with the detail of their job (the tactics) than they do with the wider picture and, despite having reached the highest levels in a business, senior managers are still prone to this – even though they know that their job is to accept the challenge of being strategic. The situation is not helped by the fact that middle and junior managers caught in this position either accept the goals they are given, even if they are unachievable, or 'sandbag' their goals to protect themselves – in other words, if they are asked for their input to the planning process they will forecast a performance that is easy to achieve so that there is little risk of failure.

In corporations which suffer from this type of management, and there are many, there is plenty of evidence to suggest that head offices just hand out goals based on purely mathematical projections – last year's numbers plus 10 per cent plus a further 10 per cent because the shareholders need better returns – and there is minimal upward input from the front line. This stems from the fact that senior management is not focused on the strategic objectives, middle management is focused on protecting their jobs, and junior management see little hope of changing anything. Unfortunately, in today's environment, this approach is likely to result in the corporation going out of business – and, if that happens, all managers will have to accept the blame.

Now, I suspect that there is a very good chance that you may actually work for a corporation which has this problem. So what can you do to break the vicious circle?

The answer is to do what you would have done if you had worked for a company with senior managers who think strategically – you must take the responsibility for determining how the objective of your team will be achieved. You must state clearly what can be achieved with your current resources, you should support this with a realistic plan, and then deliver what you say you will deliver. If you do this often enough you will eventually find that head office ask for your input on what is realistic and the objectives handed down will become achievable. The vicious circle will be broken and the company will move forward.

So how do you do this?

The answer is to **plan carefully and then work your plan**. However, a word of warning is necessary. Many managers make the mistake of embarking on this process **having already accepted** the targets – this is a major error and will trap them into the *Catch-22* situations I have just described. It is vital that you define your objectives, resources, and constraints **before** accepting the goals, especially if you are in a junior position in which you have little control over the resources available to you.

STEP 1   DEFINE THE OBJECTIVES

In most organisations the targets for the year tend to come down the line as a series of numbers that affect both sides of the equation – there are targets on the income/revenue side and there are targets on the expenses side. The first step is to sort out what the numbers mean to you and your team – to define the size and shape of the overall objective you have to achieve.

The actual size and shape of the objective depends on where it is viewed from and it is important to understand that different levels of management have different views of what has to be achieved. The Board of Directors may see the objective as the value of the company's shares and the dividend they will pay, while senior management may see it as a profit figure. The production manager is likely to see the cost of the product as his objective while the sales manager will see the total sales revenue as the key target. The assembly line manager is likely to see the total number of units assembled as his goal, while the quality manager may see the decline in the numbers of errors as his prime concern. All of these are correct and if everyone meets their targets then the company will meet its objectives.

It is vital, therefore, to clarify the task involved – exactly what are the key components that make up the objective for your team: is it a growth in revenue, an increase in sales, a decrease in expenses, or a combination of all of these? To do this you must understand the numbers that affect you – and disregard the rest. This may seem a little radical but there is little point in worrying about the share price if your primary objective is producing a given number of error-free widgets in a year.

Defining the objective for your team is your responsibility

although you would be wise to seek the assistance of your immediate superior and, possibly, your senior team members. But I suggest you do not involve too many people at this stage as incomplete information reaching junior members of the team is likely to confuse and may have a demoralising effect. After all, your responsibility is to offer leadership to your people and consensus decision-making at this stage is an abdication of that responsibility.

Once the key components have been defined and you have a very clear picture of your objective, you should obtain as much information about it as possible. This will certainly include an upward discussion with your manager to ensure that you share a common understanding of what you have to achieve. In this way you can avoid many future problems and your manager will be in a position to assist you since he will know exactly what you are trying to do. Of course, it is possible that your manager does not share your opinion or cannot accept the objective that you have defined. In this case you and he must enter into a discussion to determine his parameters and constraints and to ensure that you have a clear understanding of his objectives, and how yours fit with them. My experience has been that senior managers, as much as their junior colleagues, have seldom really focused on their objectives *in terms of the component parts* and my discussion with them has centred on identifying exactly what my team and I have to achieve as part of my manager's objectives. This usually results in a common understanding from which realistic goals can be developed.

At this stage, you should have a very clear view of what has to be done but before involving your team you need to identify your resources and understand the constraints you face. This process will tell you if the objectives are realistic and achievable for your team **as it is now** or whether you will need to obtain additional resources to carry out other activities to deliver the necessary level of performance.

STEP 2 DEFINE THE RESOURCES AND CONSTRAINTS

Your **resources** include you, your team, your budget, the time available to achieve the objective, the skills available amongst the team, marketing and other support actions being planned, your access to the market, technological support, the human resources support, and so on. This list is not exclusive and your individual situation will determine what resources you should consider – for example, if you are the manager of a production department your raw materials fall into this category, whereas if you manage a delivery section the number of vehicles will also constitute a resource.

The **constraints** you face often fall into the same categories and are generally the points of weakness in your resources. Your job at this stage is to identify actual and potential constraints and to determine their impact on your ability to achieve the objective. Beyond the obvious constraints of the budget and its impact on staff levels, training, marketing and so on, you should focus on the constraints of time and capacity (see below). These are frequently interdependent especially in such areas as sales, production, and technology.

Capacity planning – the vital exercise

Capacity planning, especially if you are a manager in a sales or production environment, is possibly your singular most important activity if you are to achieve your goals. But in undertaking this exercise, you are not trying to 'prove' the goal can or cannot be achieved – you are determining what performance can be expected given your current resources. The starting point for capacity planning is *not* the goals, but your people and the job they are *currently* doing. You need to fully understand where you are now before you can plan on going somewhere else.

This exercise is often ignored by managers – especially those who like to complain about their goals – and I can remember one group for whom the process was a turning point in their conversion to performance management. I was running a Performance Management workshop with a group of experienced front-line managers and we were talking about goals. Their general view was that senior management knew nothing about the realities of the business on the front line and the goals were pretty unachievable. On the other hand, I had previously had their senior management team on a similar seminar and knew that their approach to goals was very realistic indeed.

As we worked through the capacity planning exercise the change in attitudes was almost tangible – the group provided all the figures and the result was they realised that not only were the goals achievable but there was also spare capacity which, with the proper management approach, would produce a performance well above expectations. Almost exactly a year later, I ran a follow-up seminar at which the managers reported that they had not only hit their targets (some for the first time) but had delivered 50 per cent more than the goals which they had previously criticised as unrealistic. They identified the capacity exercise as the key to their success.

So, let us examine a typical capacity planning exercise using an office-based sales and service operation – for example, a bank, a mail-order business, or a company selling advertising space (newspaper or magazine advertising sales department). In the following example the customer visits the salespeople at their place of business (i.e. a bank), but the same process can be used for a salesforce who go out to clients (but remember to add in travelling time) and those who sell over the telephone. I have used it, with modifications, in all sorts of areas of business – in planning the capacity of a production department in a factory, in checking the staffing requirements of a policy-processing section in an insurance company, and planning the staffing levels necessary to complete an audit on time.

A Sales Capacity Planning Exercise

Answer the following questions, based on your own organisation's practices.

1. How long does the salesperson spend with a client, on average?

2. How long does a salesperson need to prepare for and record the result of a sales interview?

3. How long does a salesperson spend on service phone calls, on average?

4. How much time does the salesperson spend on administrative and service activity?

5. How long does the salesperson spend on non-business related activities, on average – i.e. coffee, toilet, gossip, etc?

6. How long does the salesperson spend on manager-imposed tasks – such as meetings, reports, and training?

7. Based on a six-hour selling day plus two hours of administration time, and taking into account non-business and manager-imposed time, how many sales interviews can a salesperson do in a day?

8. How many PROSPECTS must a salesperson interview to obtain one new relationship? (This is the closing ratio on new accounts.)

9. How many existing CLIENTS must a salesperson interview to sell one additional product to an existing client? (Closing ratio on cross-sell.)

10. Based on the closing ratios and the number of sales interviews possible per day, what is the Minimum Performance Standard (MPS) in terms of number of sales per salesperson?

11. Does the MPS for sales exceed the goals per salesperson (if so there is spare capacity) or does it fall short of the goals (in which case there is a capacity issue)?
12. Based on the closing ratios and the MPS, are there enough prospects available to the branch?
13. Based on the closing ratios and MPS, are there enough existing clients who are *real* prospects for cross-sell activity?
14. Are there *real* capacity issues or are they organisational and/or prioritisation issues?
15. What other resources are needed to address capacity and/or marketing issues (prospects, etc)?

When doing this exercise you must be careful to consider only what your people **are currently doing** – at this stage you must avoid thinking about what they **should be doing**, that comes later. In most teams there are people doing different jobs – for example, in a sales team there may be a number of salespeople plus an administrator, a secretary, and a process clerk – and you will need to carry out the capacity planning exercise for each person. This is also true if you have team members doing the same job but at different levels – for example, two salespeople, one of whom has been doing the job for five years and the other for five months.

This analysis reveals just how much time your people are spending acquiring business, doing administration, fulfilling activities to do with management, and doing nothing in terms of making money for the company. In the case of the senior line managers mentioned above, we found that administration and activities to do with management such as writing reports and attending meetings was using up around 60 per cent of the team's time – by cutting this to 20 per cent we freed up the team and they could now spend around 70 per cent of their time on acquiring business – twice as much time as before. The analysis can also open up a whole range of issues that can sidetrack you – for example, you could be tempted to start examining better ways of administering the business, of reducing non-productive time, or of handling clients, all of which are valid areas for you to examine when you have the time and after your team are well on their way to their goals.

At this point you need to consider only what you are doing now and whether this will allow you to reach your goals. If the answer is 'Yes, we can achieve our team goals doing what we are doing now,' then you can move on to an allocation of resources and start the process of achieving the objectives. Once this has begun and has picked up momentum, *then*, and only then, can you shift your focus onto all the areas that may result in your team achieving more. Remember, your prime responsibility is to achieve the team goals, not to reorganise the way the company does business.

On the other hand, if the answer is 'No, we cannot achieve our team goals based on what we are doing now,' then we have a different situation to face.

What happens when goals and performance are incompatible?

To many managers this is an all-too-familiar situation, but instead of hitting out with statements condemning the goals as unrealistic, or demanding more resources, you should consider carefully:

- what can be done to improve performance without additional resources (e.g. training, coaching, reassigning staff)
- the impact on performance that readily available, additional resources would have (e.g. additional computers, more telephone lines, better lighting, a new photocopier), and
- whether alternative tactics, but the same performance,

would enable the team to reach its goal (e.g. re-routing paperwork, cutting out unnecessary processes, telephone selling instead of direct marketing).

Having considered these points, you are then in a position to recalculate your ability to achieve the objective. However, if, having factored in all these possibilities, you are still unable to reach your goal, you at least know why and are in a position to define what can be delivered. At this point you should involve your senior manager again as he may well know of other resources that could be made available or of alternative approaches to achieving the objective. If there are none, then your manager is fully aware of what you and your team can achieve and can start the process of redistributing the goals or adjusting them downwards. (Remember, your manager has to go through a similar process in order to achieve his goals.)

Now, and only now, can you accept the goals for yourself and your team. You know what can be done and you are in a position to do it. At this stage, you can move on to planning how you will achieve the objective.

STEP 3 PLAN YOUR WORK

A leader plans his work and then works his plan – as a performance-orientated manger you must do the same. Now that you have defined the objectives, determined whether they are achievable, and know what resources are available, you can start preparing your Action Plan which will outline in detail **how** the team is going to achieve the objective.

The Action Plan

Exactly what goes into your Action Plan depends on what the objectives are but, in general terms, it should cover:

- strategy – your strategy (inclusive of tactics and actions) for achieving the objectives

- people – the people involved (human resources) and any training requirements they may have
- goals – who does what and by when (individual goals)
- monitoring – how performance is to be monitored and evaluated
- reporting – who is going to report what to whom, and when
- parameters – what actually constitutes achieving the objectives and what constitutes a deviation from plan that needs correction. For example, if one objective is to make 1,000,000 widgets within a certain specification, does making 999,750 within specification constitute a failure to meet the objective? In some circumstances it might (if it was a contract for 1,000,000), in others it might not (if it was an order to restock the store room)
- resources – other resources (i.e. budget, equipment, marketing programmes) that will be used.

This list is not exclusive, but most Action Plans can be broken down into these sections.

STEP 4 WORKING YOUR PLAN

Now that you have a clear objective and a plan for achieving it, you must work your plan.

Implementing a well-prepared plan is something that many managers find the most satisfying part of their activities, but implementation covers all aspects of working the plan and none can be left out. One thing is certain, the plan must not be put in a bottom drawer and forgotten – it is a living, working document to which you should refer frequently and against which you should check performance. The difference between managers who achieve their objectives and those who do not is that the former work their plans while the latter fight fires and forget their plans. However, you must also remember that no plan is cast in stone – if the circumstances or objectives change then the plan must be changed; if the assumptions underlying the plan are proven wrong then the plan must be altered.

A good example of this occurred just before the Gulf War as Iraq invaded Kuwait. At the time, one of my clients had a sales and local administration office based in Kuwait City, handling sales of investment products to expatriate workers based in the oil fields. Their plan was to build the sales team to three and the administrative support to two people while delivering $2 million in new investments in the year. When it became clear that Iraq would invade, the sales team actually brought in $15 million in investments while at the same time reducing their staff to one salesman – he eventually drove out of Kuwait in the last convoy of cars to reach Saudi Arabia before the border was closed.

So what is the first step?

The first step is to locate and organise your resources, most of which will have already been made available: budgets will have been signed off, equipment obtained, and so on. The second step is to assemble the team – the human resources who will actually achieve the objective. This is the subject of the following chapters.

SUMMARY POINTS

- You must take responsibility for achieving the goals and objectives of your team.
- You must clearly define the objectives.
- You must determine whether your current performance (and that of the team) will enable you to achieve the objec-

tives.

- If current performance will not allow you to achieve your objectives, then you must determine what can be achieved (and then achieve it).
- You must determine what additional resources may be needed.
- You must prepare an Action Plan – outlining the strategy and tactics for achieving the objectives and clearly showing who is responsible for achieving what by when.
- To implement the plan you must first obtain your resources.
- You must assemble your team.
- You must work your plan.

Part II
Who is going to achieve the objective?

Once you have clear objectives and a workable plan, you need to assemble and develop the people who have to carry out the plan and achieve the objectives. Most managers have already been given a team, or are appointed to lead an existing group, and few have to select a team from scratch. However, the responsibility for ensuring you have the right people doing the right job is still yours – and you must not forget that you yourself form part of the human resources dedicated to achieving your objectives.

Since you are the team leader, let us start by looking at what you have to do to be a performance manager. Once we understand ourselves in terms of our personal development and our management styles, we can then move on to looking at our team, their selection, development, and motivation.

3
Personal Development

Time management • being organised • using lists • clear desk policies • delegating • meetings • balance • Personal Time Profile • presenting the right image • your office and the way you use it • the clothes you wear • your style of communication • personal objectives • goals in your working life • private goals

THERE ARE literally hundreds of books on self-analysis, self-development, personality and the like – all of them have something to offer in helping build an understanding of ourselves, although many offer inappropriate advice and diagnosis. A colleague of mine, a creative advertising executive and very successful as a marketing director, came across a book on 'understanding yourself'. She carried out all the tests (all of which were well known and validated) and then considered the diagnosis – apparently she should never have been in marketing, certainly should never have been a manager, but should have been something like a school teacher.

These tests and questionnaires, like the ones in this book, offer insight into preferred behaviour but they are not a diagnostic tool and should not be used to determine job functions. This is an unfashionable statement to make, given the growing use of psychometrics by human resource departments and recruitment consultants. However, there is an awareness that dependence on such tests in staff selection is just as likely to result in the wrong people doing the wrong job as any other method of selection. When they are used as a guide to how a person prefers to react in a variety of situations, it is possible to use them for training and development and to help strengthen areas of weakness and exploit areas of strength.

Provided its limitations are recognised, much of the material available is very good and I recommend reading widely on the subject – always with an open mind to try and find out more about yourself. I have listed a few of my favourite self-development books in the Reading List.

From the point of view of performance management, however, we can focus on three specific areas of personal development which I have found to be very important. These areas are: **time management, presenting the right image**, and **personal objectives**.

TIME MANAGEMENT

For the performance-orientated manager there are six specific areas of time management that are vital if you are to deliver your full potential:

- being organised
- using lists
- clear desk policies
- delegating
- meetings
- balance.

Being organised

Most of us believe that we are either organised or 'totally hopeless' – in either case we are probably wrong. Being well organised is not a matter of having a highly structured process and system (although for some people this is exactly what they mean); it is more a matter of working on the most important thing, having other items in priority order, and putting things away that are finished or not needed for some time.

The key to working on the most important thing is to know what has to be done and by when. The vast majority of things that need to be done by a manager fall into the following categories: objective-achieving activities, management-imposed activities (reports, plans, etc.), staff-imposed activities (issues brought to you by your staff), fire-fighting activities (apparently urgent events that appear to need dealing with immediately), and self-imposed activities (all those things you would like to get done).

To prioritise all these activities can take some time – but it will be time well spent as it will enable you to understand what is the most important thing to do right now. But be careful in choosing the basis for the prioritisation.

Achieving objectives

Some managers assume that all activities associated with achieving the objectives must take priority. In many cases this is correct but you must be careful in identifying activities in this category – sometimes we think we are achieving the objectives while all we are actually doing is avoiding the real issues. This illusion causes us to misuse time – not to waste it, since much of what is done is of considerable value. For example, one courier company I used had a major problem delivering packages within the guaranteed time of two days and had a large backlog of undelivered packets. The cause was lack of staff; however, the manager spent five full days redesigning the dispatch process to save time (something of value to his customers). His efforts produced a vastly improved system which could be implemented some time in the future but it did not help shift the existing backlog of packages. Whilst his approach to the problem was valuable in the long term, the correct priority would have been to find more staff to shift the packages (objective-achieving activity) before tackling the redesign (self-imposed activity).

Management-imposed activities

Some managers place management-imposed activities high on their list of priorities – this is not always wise. An awful lot of reports, plans, and other management-imposed activities are designed to keep senior management informed and the penalty for failing to do so *right now* is seldom worth worrying about. The first step, therefore, is to determine the purpose of the activity, then find out why your manager wants it done before determining when it has to be completed; next decide how long it will take; and finally decide who is the most junior person in your team who can carry out the activity successfully.

In one organisation I worked in it was a corporate policy to have a monthly business letter prepared for each work unit and submitted to the next higher level of management. However, this excellent reporting and information process was seen by some managers as being so vital that they would spend days (even weeks) preparing the report. These managers saw the writing of the monthly letter as being a prime responsibility and only they could do it. This extraordinary attitude meant that some managers were spending up to 25 per cent of their working time preparing a report which their boss would spend perhaps fifteen minutes reading. Hardly the best use of valuable management time!

Staff-imposed activities

If you accept that you should be doing only your own job – carrying out your responsibilities and not those of your team members – then it is obvious that you have to delegate. You have to arrange that others in your team are given the responsibility for completing tasks which are part of their job. Oddly enough, this is something most managers find very difficult. Firstly, they are more comfortable carrying out functions with which they are familiar, and secondly they do not know how to delegate. This results in their being subjected to what is perhaps the biggest time-waster of all and thus the area that has to be most rigorously controlled – staff-imposed activity.

Staff-imposed activity is where your team members come to you and request that you do things for them. It is all too easy to say, 'Leave it with me and I'll look into it.' In just about all the situations, what you should have said is, 'I understand you have a problem – let's define it and then you can go away and find three possible solutions so that you can resolve it.' Most problems your people bring to you are really *their* responsibility and you should not take it away from them – by leaving them with the responsibility, you will allow them to develop and you will have protected your time.

Fighting fires

For most managers, the most difficult area to prioritise is that of fighting fires. Throughout the working week there is a constant stream of apparently urgent items that need your immediate attention and frequently take up a great deal of time. Dealing with these issues is referred to as fire-fighting. However, my experience is that few urgent items are that important. The vast majority seem designed to use up valuable time but, because dealing with urgent issues (emergencies!?) appears exciting and we all love rushing around being busy, we put aside important (non-urgent!) issues and allow ourselves to be sucked into the whirlwind activity of fire-fighting.

Let me pass on the advice I was given about fire-fighting. What is urgent for one person is seldom urgent for another and, as a manager, your responsibility is to set priorities. Whenever a member of your team comes to you with an emergency (something urgent from his point of view) you invite him into your office, you sit down, and you ask him to define the problem and to outline the solutions that could lead to a successful resolution. Such an approach generally results in a calmer and clearer view of the matter. If it still appears you have a fire, then consider what the result would be of *not* dealing with it – experience has shown that not dealing with the apparent 'emergency' until at least a couple of hours has passed generally results in not having to deal with it at all and the damage is limited to the raised level of excitement amongst a few members of the team.

Using lists

Let's go back and look at the practicalities of being organised. The first step is to write down everything that you have to get done and the date for completion. The next stage is to determine how long each item will take. These two steps will give you a guide to the order or priority. Once you have the roughly prioritised list you should examine each item carefully to see whether:

(a) it really needs to be done – if not, put it on a 'nice to do' list, and

(b) it is your responsibility to do it – if not, delegate it to the right person, along with instructions on how it could be done and when it has to be done by.

Your list will now have been reduced to those things that *are* your responsibility. They can then be reorganised and each item given a number in order of priority.

Now rewrite the list in the correct order – this is the order in which you will carry out the tasks and in this way you will always be working on the most important thing at that moment.

I suggest you decide how many items you can complete today and make a separate list of these, select all the documents you need for the first item and put all others aside and start work. When you have finished an item, cross it off the list and put the documents and other information away – that job is now over. Even if you do not get everything done on that day's list you will have worked on the most important.

At the end of each day, prepare a list for the following day starting with the unfinished items from the current list and adding in those from the main list.

'But,' I hear you say, 'what happens if the next day is full of meetings or genuine emergencies?' The answer is that you deal with the meetings and genuine emergencies, but when these have been completed always go back to the list. Over time, new items get added to the list and new priorities are raised – sometimes this means that items get pushed down the ranking and occasionally they get transferred to the 'nice to do' list, but your main list will always contain the most important things that you need to do.

I use this system all the time. My daily list generally has no more than two or three items on it, my main list seldom has more than ten items on it, and my 'nice to do' list tends to have around twenty-five items (I transfer them to the main list whenever I can). The lists are all kept on pieces of paper in a loose-leaf file (for the last few years I have used a Filofax for this purpose but any file will do) – this gives me the pleasure of physically crossing out completed items and throwing away completed lists.

My lists for today are as follows:

Actions for today	*Priority actions*	*Nice to do*
Telephone bank	Write project report	Rearrange office
Meet client X	Complete Chapter 3	Establish project track
Corrections to spreadsheet	Prepare survey	Learn new programme
	Job Spec for new consultant	
Dinner with family	Plan Chapter 4	
	Chase G for report	

Using a priority list and working on only one thing at a time generally results in less paper around the office since you only have out the documents on which you are working. When the job is complete (or, if the job is large and requires some work on it over a period of days, completed to the required stage), the papers are put away – this leaves a clear working area for the next job.

'But,' I hear you say, 'I always have a number of projects on the go. How can I work on just one thing at a time.' Actually, it is not possible to work on two things at the same time – it is only possible to work on one, the other items will be temporarily put aside. In these circumstances you should determine what the next thing is that needs doing **on each project.** Having done that, you have to decide which action *must* be carried out next and in this way you can prioritise your activities. As a consultant I normally have three or four major projects on the go for different clients and each project has a priority list and then I have a master list from which I work.

Clear desk policies

As great deal is talked about clear desks –statements such as 'An untidy desk shows an unorganised mind,' and 'Only have out the paper you are working on,' are found in almost all books on time management – but most of the dictums are ideals which many managers just cannot put into practice. Many jobs require lots of bits of information to be available at the same time, generally written on lots of different bits of paper. In these circumstances, a tidy desk is often impossible.

My approach is somewhat different. I believe you should have on your desk only the papers **that relate to the job being carried out at that moment** and that all other paper and documents should be put away – this includes papers relating to the job in hand but not required at that time. This reduces the disorder and minimises the risk of loose sheets getting lost amongst unrelated papers. The important thing is to put away all the documents and papers once the job has been finished or finished for the day. To me, a clear desk policy refers to the fact that the desk is cleared after each job.

Delegating

For the proper management of your time, and to avoid time-wasting staff-imposed activities, you need to delegate to others all activities that are not your responsibility. The key to this is contained in the following rules:

1. decide who in your team is the most junior person capable of carrying out the activity successfully
2. instruct them on what has to be done, the standards that have to be achieved, and the deadline for completion
3. ensure they understand the task and have the skills and knowledge to complete it
4. check and control progress, either

   - by requesting the person to decide on actions, carry them out, and then tell you what they have done,

   or

   - by requiring them to determine a course of action and to get your permission before proceeding.

The choice of check and control will depend on your level of confidence in their ability to work without supervision.

For a simple explanation of the art of delegating (and thus freeing up your time for more valuable activities) you should read *The One Minute Manager Meets the Monkey* by Kenneth Blanchard, William Oncken and Hal Burrows.

Meetings

Here is another big time-waster. The bigger the corporation, the greater the number of meetings, the more time is wasted. Some companies even have meetings about meetings. Most corporations have meetings that produce no results of any sort other than the emotional satisfaction of those involved in the meeting. Meetings are even held just for the sake of holding a meeting – meetings are a source of power: he who calls the meeting has the power. Some meetings are useful, of course, and some meetings are important, but most could be replaced by a quick telephone call, a conference call using speaker phones or conference call system, or even by one person taking action and then informing others. So, for what reason should you hold a meeting? The answer is when you need to

- discuss,
- train,
- decide, or
- motivate.

You should hold a meeting whenever you have major **news or information** to impart to an individual or to your team **which will raise questions**. Obviously, news and information can often be most easily transmitted via a memo, but if the news or information is going to cause the recipient to ask questions then it is better to hold a meeting. In this way, everyone involved hears the news the same way (probably backed up by a memo) and they all have an opportunity to ask questions and have points clarified.

Similarly, if **training** needs to be delivered, this should be done face-to-face, either in a group or one-to-one. In either case, hold a meeting.

If you wish an individual or the whole team to reach a **decision** on some action then again, hold a meeting. In this way everyone is involved in the decision-making process and will accept the resulting decision.

Finally, if you wish to **motivate** an individual or a group this is best done face-to-face because much of the motivation will be delivered through your enthusiasm – something that cannot be conveyed adequately through a memo. Into this category fall those meetings, where the objective is to build team spirit – a meeting just to get the team together in one place (for example; a sales meeting or management meeting of a geographically spread-out team).

Whatever the reason for the meeting, there are certain rules you should follow if it is to be successful and not a waste of time:

1 Have a very clearly defined objective for the meeting – something that has to be achieved – and convey this to each person attending.

2 Have an agenda – a running order to ensure that all the important items are dealt with. I have found the most effective agenda states the objective of the meeting and has perhaps only three critical items on it. These are the items that *must* be discussed and resolved. Following these there may be a group of less important items that can be covered if time permits.

3 Circulate the agenda when calling the meeting – this allows everyone to prepare themselves and their contribution since they know what is to be discussed. Try to allow a little time (around five working days) between circulating the agenda and the actual meeting – this allows preparation without allowing pre-meeting meetings to be held.

4 Start and finish all meetings at the times specified. If all the agenda items have not been covered, call another meeting or delegate the topics to sub-groups or individuals.

5 Do not allow interruptions from outside the meeting (i.e. telephone calls) and do not allow those attending to do anything other than focus on the subject under discussion.

6 Stick to the agenda – the subjects for discussion are those on the agenda, other subjects belong in other meetings.

7 Always, always summarise the items covered, the decisions reached, and the actions that have to be taken. Each person, on leaving the meeting, should know who has to take what actions by which dates.

8 Circulate the minutes of the meeting in headline form (i.e. key items and key decisions with names of those who must take action) within one or two working days to every person who attended.

9 Always follow up on decisions and actions – this is your responsibility.

Meetings should be interesting, informative, decisive, motivating and productive. The people attending should look forward to the meeting even if it is going to be difficult for them. They should never feel that the meeting was a waste of time.

Balance

The final area of time management that is vital to your success is getting the balance right. The balance between goal-achieving and tension-relieving, between family and work, between stress and relaxation, between good habits and bad, and between all the responsibilities of your job.

We all know of the managers who are devoted to their job, working late and at weekends, and even bringing work home. And we all know their families: trying to keep quiet because mummy or daddy is working or just ignoring the workaholic parent's existence and living their own lives. And we have all heard their claim that 'I'm doing it all for them.' What a sorry picture, and what a lie. Workaholics do not work for the benefit of their families, but to satisfy some deep need of their own – if they cared about their family they would ensure they spent more time with them doing things together as a family. They lose touch with their friends, who start telephoning less often. Workaholics tend also to be dangerous to their own health and to the health of their company – living with stress and not taking the time to relax and unwind causes raised blood pressure, deterioration in the immune system, making the body more susceptible to illness, and can (and frequently does) lead to heart problems, especially in men, all of which have serious consequences for ourselves, our family, and our company.

We need to ensure there is a balance between the time we spend working (and working towards our goals) and the time we spend relieving tension, relaxing, and being with our friends or family. For me, the time spent with my family gives me a break from my work-related thoughts and allows me to consider new ideas, new approaches, and new viewpoints – in fact, turning my conscious thoughts to non-work activity allows my sub-conscious to get on with dealing with work matters. This is not to say there will not be times when we have to work long hours, over weekends, or bring work home – but these should be rare and vital occasions and not a regular part of life. If they are necessary, then explain to the family what you are doing and gain their support. When the pressure is off and the job completed, take extra time with friends and family and extra time for yourself.

Only you can achieve this balance. Your colleagues, your boss, your friends and family can only advise when they think things are out of balance. It is up to you to manage your time effectively so that you deliver your goals, both at work and in your private life. The key is to work smarter – not harder. There is a fixed amount of time available in any day and we should use it wisely.

The *Personal Time Profile* questionnaire on pages 44 to 57 will allow you to check your time management and to find out more about how to control your time. This is reproduced with permission from Sandy Ellvers-Dix.

Personal Time Profile

An assessment of the considerations and priorities which affect an individual's management of time

Instructions for completion

On the following pages, you will find 75 questions relating to some aspects of Time Management. Please read the questions and decide on one of the following answers.

1 Rarely, if not at all.
2 Sometimes.
3 Usually.

Write in the box next to the questions the number **1** if it is 'rarely, if not at all', the number **2** if it is 'sometimes' and the number **3** if it is 'usually'.

When you have finished all the questions, you can add up the total for each of the five columns on all pages of the questionnaire.

1 – Rarely, if not at all/2 – Sometimes/3 – Usually	A	B	C	D	E
1 Do you prepare a daily plan?					
2 Do you find it difficult falling asleep at night because you are constantly thinking about work?					
3 Do you try to complete one job at a time, instead of flitting from task to task?					
4 Do you invent reasons and look for excuses for not taking action on a difficult problem?					
5 Do you maintain an up-to-date and realistic specification of your own job?					
Page total					

Personal Development 45

1 – Rarely, if not at all/2 – Sometimes/3 – Usually

	A	B	C	D	E
6 Do you say 'no' and avoid getting personally involved in problems that can be ignored, postponed or delegated?				☐	
7 Do you feel there are not enough hours in the day to do what you want?					☐
8 Do you carry out an accurate and realistic check (a period of a week or a month) of exactly how your time is spent?	☐				
9 Do you find yourself doing more than one task at a time, e.g. talking to colleagues while writing notes on another subject?					☐
10 Do you know the key areas where you must achieve results in order to do your job properly?	☐				
11 Do you have a regular time each day for dealing with correspondence?		☐			
12 When you are interrupted, do you give the individual a time limit?				☐	
13 Can you place various jobs into subject groups so that you are not changing from one area to another?	☐				
14 Do you aim to clear your incoming post the first time you handle it?		☐			
15 When you are busy with a deadline and someone interrupts you, do you explain why you are busy and arrange to speak to them later?				☐	
16 Do you know what you want to be doing in five years' time?	☐				
Page total					

1 – Rarely, if not at all/2 – Sometimes/3 – Usually

	A	B	C	D	E
17 Do you find yourself so preoccupied that you have forgotten things, double-booked or missed appointments?					☐
18 Do you make time in your diary for working on specific projects and assignments?	☐				
19 Do you wait until the pressure is on before working on a difficult assignment?			☐		
20 Do you pretend to listen to other people and their views, but you are really preoccupied with your own thoughts?					☐
21 Do you know the time of day you work most effectively and therefore use this for working on your most difficult tasks?	☐				
22 When you are asked by a superior to do extra work, which you don't think you have time for, do you explain your problems, giving evidence that if extra work is to be done then you will have to give less attention to other work?				☐	
23 Do you take half measures in order to avoid or delay difficult or unpleasant action?			☐		
24 Do you find yourself continually dealing with one crisis after another?					☐
25 Do you regularly review your objectives and goals with your boss?	☐				
26 Do you take action to stop people sending you paperwork which you do not need?		☐			
27 Are you unable to have interests and hobbies outside the work environment?					☐
28 When someone has done work for you incorrectly, do you correct it yourself and say nothing?				☐	
Page total					

Personal Development

1 – Rarely, if not at all / 2 – Sometimes / 3 – Usually

	A	B	C	D	E
29 Do you allow too many interruptions and crises to interfere with your accomplishing important tasks?			☐		
30 Do you throw away as much paperwork as you can, instead of automatically filing it?		☐			
31 Do you plan your day the night before?	☐				
32 Do you avoid forthright answers when pressed for an unpleasant decision?			☐		
33 Do you find that you are having difficulty in meeting deadlines for your job?					☐
34 When casual visitors drop in to your office, do you have difficulty getting rid of them?				☐	
35 Do you prioritise your daily list of 'Things to do'?	☐				
36 Do you scan reports, magazines, etc., for relevant information and read in detail only material which is important to you?		☐			
37 Do you feel guilty whenever you try to relax?				☐	
38 Have you been guilty of neglecting follow-up aspects of important action plans?		☐			
39 Do you take care not to over-extend your coffee or lunch breaks?		☐			
40 Do you discourage others from trying to leave their problems with you?				☐	
41 Do you know what your goals and objectives are for the next 12 months?	☐				
42 Do you try to get other people to do unpleasant assignments for you?		☐			
Page total					

48 Managing for Performance

1 – Rarely, if not at all/2 – Sometimes/3 – Usually	A	B	C	D	E
43 Do you discourage your colleagues from wasting time with office chit-chat when you are working on an important task?				☐	
44 Prior to a meeting, do you ensure that there is a start and finish time?	☐				
45 Do you call meetings only when the situation cannot be handled in any better way?		☐			
46 Do you schedule important or difficult jobs too late in the day, or constantly take work home with you?				☐	
47 Prior to making a telephone call, do you write down the phone number, who it is you wish to speak to, or an alternative person if they are not there, and what you want to say?	☐				
48 Do you suffer from frequent headaches and/or digestive complaints?					☐
49 Do you attend only those meetings which deal with issues that directly affect your job?		☐			
50 Do you like to clear your desk of all minor and routine tasks before commencing a tough assignment?			☐		
51 Do you cut off your telephone when you are holding an important meeting in your office and brief someone to discourage unscheduled visitors?		☐			
52 Do you note down a quiet time in your daily schedule?	☐				
53 Do you find yourself getting easily irritated if things don't go well?					☐
Page total					

Personal Development

1 – Rarely, if not at all/2 – Sometimes/3 – Usually	A	B	C	D	E
54 Do you, before leaving the office, make a note of any tasks not yet completed for inclusion on the next day's action list?		✓			
55 Do you block out time in your diary for dealing with routine matters?	✓				
56 Do you ask for more time to think when pressed for a decision?					
57 Do you give precedence to matters that are important but not urgent over matters that are urgent?		✓			
58 Do you use minor ailments as an excuse to stay away from the office when unpopular decisions need to be taken?			✓		
59 Do you find it difficult to concentrate in meetings?				✓	
60 Do you make full use of your diary for planning dates, appointments, meetings, goals and completion of tasks?	✓				
61 Do you, when dealing with the post, keep picking up pieces of paper and putting them down again without taking some kind of action?			✓		
62 Are you unable to regularly plan and take time for holidays?				✓	
63 Do you use a checklist to keep your telephone conversations to the point and avoid digression on non-business matters?				✓	
64 Do you blame your boss for your own indecisiveness by saying that he/she is never around when you want to discuss important matters?		✓			
Page total					

1 – Rarely, if not at all / 2 – Sometimes / 3 – Usually

	A	B	C	D	E
65 Do you have an efficient reminder system?	☐				
66 Do you keep your desk clear of all papers except those on which you are working?		☐			
67 Do you allow meetings to end without decisions being taken because you are afraid to offend a powerful individual or faction?			☐		
68 Do you have no sense of achievement when you leave work at the end of your day?					☐
69 Do you build in flexibility when planning your time, allowing time for possible interruptions?	☐				
70 Do you place a 'Do Not Disturb' sign in a prominent place?		☐			
71 Do you sometimes feel bored with your job?					☐
72 Does your diary contain a system for retaining relevant data to help you achieve your key objectives?	☐				
73 When someone makes an appointment to see you, do you ascertain the importance of the meeting and how long it will take?				☐	
74 Do you break down large tasks into smaller ones that can be handled in shorter time periods?		☐			
75 Do you organise meetings to provide you with further information – even though you have enough already?			☐		
Page total					

Score sheet

To produce a total score for this questionnaire, you must first add up the totals from all pages of the questionnaire. This can be done on the chart alongside.

Page	A	B	C	D	E
1					
2					
3					
4					
5					
6					
7 Total					

KEY ACTION AREAS

A is Goal setting and Planning
B is Time principles
C is Procrastination
D is Assertiveness
E is Coping with stress

KEY ACTION AREAS

A	B	C	D	E
—60	—45		—30	
	—40	—5	—25	—5
—50	—35	—10	—20	—10
—40	—30	—15	—20	—15
	—25	—20	—15	—20
—30	—20	—25		—25
—20	—15	—30	—10	—30
	—10	—35	—5	—35
—10	—5	—40		—40
		—45		—45

If any of your scores are in this sector of the graph, then congratulations. You seem to have control of that particular key area.

If your scores are in this sector, then you are on the right track for controlling that area. However, review the key actions on the following pages and see if there are some actions that may help you further.

If any of your scores are in this sector of the graph, then be aware that you are in the danger area and need to take immediate action. Read the key actions for the relevant key areas and try to implement them as soon as possible.

Now turn to the relevant action area to find out your action plan for improving your time management

On the following pages you will be given explanations of the five Key Action Areas.

Please read them carefully and ask yourself honestly – 'Do I implement these time principles or could they become part of my Action Plan for the future?' Next to each Key Action is a box. Tick the box when you have completed that action.

The effective management of time requires careful consideration of five major factors. They are:

1 Goal setting and Planning
2 Useful time principles
3 Procrastination
4 Assertiveness
5 Stress

Goal setting and Planning

Goal setting and Planning is the singularly most important area for managing time.

Before you can manage your time, you need to have a clear idea of what you want to manage and why. The 'why' can encompass your goals and objectives not only for today, but for the next three months, twelve months or even three to five years. You cannot plan today without knowing how that one simple unit of time fits into the bigger picture.

Once you know why you are doing something, then you have to plan 'how'. This means taking your goals and breaking them down into key areas where you want to achieve results and then setting yourself standards for achieving those results.

This information should be contained in your job description.

Key actions:

- Make sure you have a diary system to help you keep track of your day-to-day activities. It should also contain a Key Results Area section, which provides the relevant data to help you to achieve your goals and objectives. ☐

- Agree Key Result Areas and standards with your boss. ☐

- Regularly review your job description with your boss, preferably once every three months. ☐

- Block out periods of time in your diary when you work most effectively, for dealing with priority tasks. Avoid booking people-associated activities such as meetings, visitors, etc., in that important time period. ☐

- Make sure you know the start and finish times of meetings so that you can plan your time effectively before and afterwards. ☐

- Before leaving work, plan your next day's activities and prioritise your list of things to do. ☐

Time principles

If you were to read all the books and watch all the training films about time management, you would find that they all say very much the same things. Good time management principles are universal and basic common sense. If these principles are practised, then you will be a long way down the road to improving your time management.

Key actions:

- Block out a regular time each day in your diary for dealing with routine matters such as correspondence, and try to clear your incoming post the first time you handle it. ☐

- Try to complete one job at a time and avoid the 'butterfly' approach of flitting from task to task. ☐

- Throw away as much paperwork as you can instead of automatically filing it. Also try to save trees by stopping people sending you paperwork you do not need. ☐

- Attend a Rapid Reading course to help improve your skills of scanning reports, journals, magazines, etc. for relevant information and reading with high retention the detail which is important to you. ☐

- When organising meetings, make sure that the situation cannot be handled in some other more efficient way. Also make sure you attend only those meetings which deal with issues that directly affect your job. ☐

- Keep your desk clear of all papers except those on which you are working. Try to avoid all possible distractions which irrelevant paperwork might cause. ☐
- Before leaving the office, make a note of any tasks not yet completed for inclusion in the next day's action list. ☐
- Telephones are great time-wasters. Try to switch it off or get someone else to intercept the call when you need a quiet time to concentrate or are involved in a meeting. ☐
- Take care not to extend coffee or lunch breaks. ☐
- Before making a phone call:
  1. write down the number;
  2. who you want to speak to;
  3. an alternative person if your original choice is unavailable;
  4. the key objectives of the call.
  Using a three-minute egg timer, try to keep all calls within that time limit. ☐
- Place a 'Do Not Disturb – Person at Work' sign in a prominent position. ☐
- Break large tasks down into smaller parts. It is rather like eating a loaf of bread – 'one slice at a time'. ☐

Procrastination

If we were to identify the biggest time-waster in our lives, all we would have to do is look in the mirror. As the proverb says, 'Procrastination is the thief of time.' Some of us work better under pressure and need the adrenalin to achieve results. This can, however, cause unnecessary stress.

There are some key actions to help us overcome this problem.

Key actions:

- If you have a difficult or unpleasant task to undertake, write down the start date in your diary. Tell other people that you intend to start this task then. Committing yourself on paper or verbally helps motivate you into action. ☐

- Note down due dates in your diary for projects to be completed. Give yourself a countdown of time, e.g. two weeks before the 'XYZ' report is due, one week before the 'XYZ' report is due. ☐
- Note down in your diary target dates for the follow-up aspects of important action plans. ☐
- Schedule unpleasant tasks at the time of day when you are at your best and more able to tackle those tasks. ☐
- Prioritise your 'Things to Do' list into:
  A – important tasks, must be done by you today;
  B – not so important tasks, with no immediate time limit;
  C – minor and routine tasks.
  Make sure you start on the As and Bs and do not let the C tasks take up your time. 'C' tasks make you feel good only because you can tick them off easily. ☐
- Ensure meetings end with an action plan and a clear understanding of who is to undertake what action. ☐
- Whenever possible, take the DIN approach – 'Do It Now'. Too much analysis can lead to paralysis. ☐
- If you have a large and overwhelming task to deal with, then break it down into smaller parts and deal with those smaller parts one at a time. ☐

Assertiveness

One of the biggest time problems people face is their inability to say 'no' to the requests of others. Two main reasons can influence them. It could be, first, the fear of those in a more senior position, or second, not wanting to be badly thought of by refusing a request. An understanding of assertiveness can make people appreciate that situations such as saying 'no' can be coped with in a positive manner, leaving an individual without the feeling of guilt. The aim of assertiveness is to achieve what you want, whilst maintaining the self-respect of yourself and others.

Key actions:

- Attend an assertiveness course. If that is not possible, read *Assertiveness At Work* by David Stubbs. ☐

- Use the broken-record technique for refusing requests. This is the skill of being persistent, saying what you want over and over again without getting angry, irritated or loud. When saying 'no', give a good reason why and work out a compromise if necessary. ☐

- Stand up when casual visitors drop in. Do not give them the opportunity to get comfortable. ☐

- Give interruptions a time limit. Say 'I can give you seven minutes' rather than the standard five or ten minutes. ☐

- Do not take on everyone's problems. Reflectively listen to their problems and encourage people to focus on their own solutions. ☐

- When correcting someone else's sub-standard work, be sure to highlight any positive points before asking them how they plan to improve the standard. ☐

- Do not allow others to manage your diary. Keep the time you work most effectively free of appointments instigated by others. Book them into your diary at a time that is convenient for **you**. ☐

- Before making a telephone call, write down the objective of the call and stick to the point. ☐

Stress

Do you work to live or live to work? Good time management should provide you with a good quality of life at work and at home. If you have scored highly in this section, then it is important to undertake the following actions to ensure that you do not drive yourself out of a job.

Key actions:

- Try and implement the actions in sections A (Goal setting and Planning) and B (Time principles). ☐

- Block out time in your diary for some time off – a one- or two-week holiday or a long weekend. A change is as good as a rest. ☐

- Allow yourself fifteen minutes a day to practise progressive relaxation techniques. ☐

- Make sure you take a lunch break and go outside for a walk if possible. ☐

- If you do not have an interest or hobby outside the work environment, then take one up. ☐

- If you feel you are physically below par, make an appointment with your doctor for a check-up. Your doctor will be able to advise you regarding diet and exercise. ☐

- A crisis is an unexpected event that requires a major decision to be made quickly. Identify and write down those types of crises that keep occurring and organise a contingency plan for the future. ☐

    Checklist of action for coping with a crisis:
    1. Is it my problem?
    2. Do I have the facts?
    3. Has this happened before?
    4. What are my objectives?
    5. What are my priorities?
    6. Make and implement a plan.
    7. Communicate to relevent parties.

Reproduced with permission from Sandy Ellvers-Dix

PRESENTING THE RIGHT IMAGE

In terms of being an effective manager, the image you project is far more important than many people believe. The way you are perceived affects the way people react to you and determines your effectiveness – and the way you are perceived is a reflection of the image you present. It is vital, therefore, that you project the right image – the image of a professional and effective manager.

But what makes up this image?

In simple terms it is based on the way you behave, the way you dress, and the way you communicate. But we can go further – it is also the positioning of your desk in the office, where you sit (and where other people sit) in a meeting, your attitude towards time-keeping, towards business appointments, and towards meetings.

Some years ago a book was published concerning the way organisations work. In it the author suggested that the location of a manager's office and the layout of furniture in that office was a clear indication of the manager's power. The higher up the ladder you were, the more important it was to have a corner office on an upper floor. Your desk would be situated across a corner furthest from, but facing, the door – thus forcing a visitor to walk the greatest distance under your watchful eye, or, if the author was to be believed, not under your watchful eye as you would certainly not look until they reached your desk, thus conducting a power play to exert your position. Furthermore, your visitor would have had to get past one, or even two, secretaries who would have kept him waiting just a few minutes past the time of the appointment. All this just to show how important you were – to project an image of power.

The truly powerful manager does not have to resort to this sort of behaviour – the manager's legitimate position in the organisation and own sense of self-worth and self-confidence will establish any 'power' *vis-à-vis* others. But 'power' is the wrong term – although it is reasonably accurate – since it suggests control, strength, and force. We, as performance managers, should be more interested in the impact we have on others. After all, it is rather unlikely that you or I would have 'power' over the management levels above us and yet we must be able to 'manage upwards', we must be able to have an impact at higher levels so that we can achieve our objectives.

This impact is derived from the way we walk, talk, move,

dress, our manners, our attitude, the way we listen, the way we respond. All these, and more, help attract a response. Our behaviour governs the behaviour directed towards us. If we are angry then it attracts fear which is often covered by anger – thus, anger attracts angry behaviour in response. Calm behaviour attracts calmness in response. If you are always interrupting people when they talk, they will eventually stop talking to you. If you have a disinterested or uninterested attitude towards someone they will feel unwanted and will turn to someone else.

Since we are primarily interested in managing people – getting the best performance from those around us – there are a few key areas which we should look at in greater detail:

- your office
- your clothes
- your communication style.

Your office and the way you use it

Quite often it is impossible, or at least very difficult, to arrange an office in any other way than the 'traditional', desk-facing-the-door layout. However, occasionally it may be possible to change things around and, if you can, then you can achieve some surprising results.

The first thing you should do, before making changes to the layout of your office, is to decide exactly what your office is for. 'Oh, come on,' I hear you say, 'we all know what an office is for.' But do we? Offices have a variety of functions – as places to work and think, places in which to hold meetings, places in which to interview people, places to escape to – and only you can decide the primary function of your office.

My office is a work location. I use it to work on the computer, make and receive telephone calls, study documents, and so on. I almost never hold a meeting in my office – when people come to see me we move to a different room with comfortable, informal furniture or we sit around a conference table in yet a third room – as a result, my office is functional. I have a desk on which the computer, printer, and telephone and fax machine sit. This desk faces a wall (firstly, a blank wall is less distracting than a window or the sight of a corridor and secondly, it stops things falling off the back) and is used entirely for working on the computer and talking on the telephone.

I have a second desk which faces the opposite wall. This one is generally clear of everything except a desk light and is used for studying documents and working with papers. The rest of the room is taken up with filing systems, bookcases, and some seating for anyone who happens to want to come in and sit down (not many do and the seat is generally unused).

This office is very different from the one I had when I was working as an internal consultant with a large bank. There my office was frequently a meeting room as well as a work area. In fact, the nature of my work meant that meetings in my office were the primary activity. Because of this, I had a desk (again, facing a wall) on which the computer and telephone were located, various filing systems tucked into corners, and a large round table with a number of chairs. Thus, meetings – which took up probably 60 per cent of the day – took place around the table which dominated the room, and I worked in one corner.

The financial controller at the bank used his office purely for work and never held meetings there, with the result that he had no chairs for visitors and his L-shaped desk occupied a substantial part of the room and was covered with computers and all the equipment of his business activity. From a visitor's point of view, it was very uninviting but it served the purpose – the whole effect was to say: this is strickly a work area.

Whether you can change your office around or not is a matter of practicality. How you use your office is a matter of choice and there are a few general rules which, if followed, allow the office to be useful in terms of performance management.

No barriers
If you have to have your desk facing the room, ensure that it is kept clear of unnecessary papers and equipment. It is especially important that no objects are aligned across the back of the desk – remember, the back of the desk is furthest away from you but it it nearest to your visitors and objects placed there act as a barrier. Psychologically, such barriers are perceived as being there to protect the manager and thus produce negative reactions from visitors.

Think back to the last time you were a visitor and were 'seen' across a crowded desk – how did you feel about having to move his papers to put down your own and were you comfortable moving the picture of his wife and children so that you had somewhere to put a coffee cup? Or, worse still, when you sat down what were your feelings when you had to try and see him from behind a stack of in-trays?

Welcome
Always get up from behind your desk and come to meet your visitor. Show him or her to a seat. Make them feel that visiting you is not something to be afraid of. If possible, sit on the same side of the desk as your visitor. Better still, of course, don't sit at the desk at all.

Courtesy
Don't allow telephone calls or other outside interruptions to disturb the meeting – tell callers you will call back and ask your team to interrupt only if the place is on fire – all other reasons are not sufficiently important for a meeting to be interrupted. Equally, never make phone calls during a meeting except when they relate directly to the matter under discussion. This attitude suggests to your people that when they meet with you in your office it is important and private. This sort of courtesy will encourage your people to talk openly and honestly and will help develop positive communications.

Accessibility

My general rule is that my door is always open. I close the door only when I am with someone (privacy and courtesy to them) or am working on something that needs total concentration. When my door is closed my team know not to interrupt except in a real emergency. If you also follow this rule, remember to open the door again when the closed door is no longer needed.

(Doors are rather a problem in other countries – the Germans like to have their office doors closed at all times so do the Dutch. The Spaniards keep theirs open as do the Greeks – even to the extent of forgetting to close them when appropriate. According to the circumstances, play this a little carefully.)

The clothes you wear

There are two considerations to take into account:

- the 'accepted' style of clothing for the job and the company
- your personal style.

There is a well-known American merchant bank which had a strict dress code laying down that all junior managers (and all senior managers, for all I know) should dress in white shirts, dark ties, very dark or black suits with a minimum of stripe, and black shoes. Hair length was also governed by the rule and had to be kept off the collar and above the ears. No tie pins were allowed, cuff links had to be plain and wrist watches had to be unostentatious. The rules there, although more relaxed now, are still applied and anyone who breaks them is likely to damage their career or to be dismissed.

A little harsh and unrealistic, you may think, but the company had built its reputation on the sober professional image and saw its dress code as an essential adjunct to maintain that reputation. It is interesting to note that they have never been short of quality people applying for the very limited number of vacancies that occur.

Such dress codes, which are common in many businesses, are essentially male-orientated and originated in the 1950s and 60s, frequently stemming from the views of senior managers of the 'old school' who had had a military background. The arrival of women in managerial positions in the 1970s and 80s presented a problem, both for the companies and for the women – a problem resolved by the women themselves who adopted the female version of the male dress code. Dark suits were worn with white blouses and many women even went so far as to wear some sort of dark 'tie'.

By the late 1980s 'power dressing' had developed, with women's business attire mimicking the male outfits by the use of padded shoulders, longer jackets, and severe skirts all designed to present a more 'aggressive/assertive', male-type image. Jewellery, when worn, was always discreet and the whole effect was almost a denial of femininity. (Some women even went so far as to adopt inappropriate male language and male prejudices in an attempt to appear more like their male colleagues.)

Fortunately, there is now a move away from 'power dressing' and women are again selecting outfits that, although 'sober' and 'businesslike', reflect their personalities and femininity Personally, I applaud this trend as it allows women to be themselves and bring to their role the professionalism and intelligence which allow them to be excellent managers without the distraction of inappropriate behaviour and dress.

The Japanese manufacturing companies are also well known for their dress codes – everyone, from the most senior manager down to the lowest-paid line worker, wears exactly the same uniform overalls. In this case the reasoning is to build team spirit and company loyalty and to eliminate the 'class' distinction between managers and workers.

And, of course, there are many companies in manufacturing, construction, engineering, and the like who impose a strict dress code based on personal safety.

Whatever reason the company has for having a dress code (whether explicit or implicit), it would be foolish to challenge it. To do so would be to be marked as a rebel, not a team player, 'not one of us'. To successfully challenge a dress code requires you to have proven abilities that are highly prized by the organisation and a level of self-confidence that will sustain you through the ostracism that frequently is the lot of the rebel.

It is worth noting that sometimes it is not the company that applies a dress code but the customers. There is a wide range of professions and businesses which appear to have a dress code based on the company's understanding of the perceptions of the customer. For example, clients are generally thought to prefer their solicitors to dress in sober suits (except for the country solicitor who is expected to be in tweeds or a tweed jacket and flannels.) Bank customers are thought to trust bank managers more when they are dressed in dark suits. Passengers are more relaxed and confident when the pilot of the aircraft is seen to wear a uniform with gold braid.

Although a suit is generally acceptable wherever you go in business, there are some anomalies – some computer companies actively encourage their people to wear jeans and sweatshirts (although it is an interesting fact that the same companies employ sales people who have been found to be more successful when dressed in a suit). Advertising agencies and other creative organisations are well known for their casual approach to dress – although again, it is a little difficult to present an image of credibility while wearing sandals, jeans, and a T-shirt saying *Have a nice day* during a presentation of a multi-million-pound campaign to the soberly dressed directors of a blue-chip company. Foreign cultures also play a part – Germans and Dutch business people are either very soberly dressed or are to be found in slacks and brightly coloured jackets. The Italians favour shiny material for their suits while the Americans, if not in the international dark suit, are often in loud checks. The Japanese are invariably in dark suits, while the Australians favour light colours and short-sleeved shirts.

As a manager and a leader, you have to present the right image to your people, and the right image of your company to your customers – and your personal style has to be put aside unless it satisfies all the criteria associated with your job. Let me use myself as an example: when I was operating as an internal consultant for one of my clients (a large international bank), I had to lead the sales team, meet the company's customers, and generally appear to be a good team player – this required me to wear a suit and tie all day, the very image of a banker. Later, I undertook another contract with the same client, but this time as an external consultant. It was important that I was *not* seen as a banker but as an advisor, an outsider, as different. To achieve this, I reverted to a style closer to my personal style (casual clothes and definitely no ties) and took to wearing jackets and trousers rather than a suit – I did, however, wear a tie as this seemed appropriate. This choice of clothes identified me as an outsider, but also as a professional, a person called in to assist but not to challenge or threaten anyone's position.

Finally, whatever clothing style you have to adopt for your role as a manager, always ensure it is of good quality, well cut, and well made (all of which will give you confidence) – and clean. Stains and dirt happen to all of us but it shows lack of awareness about our image if we fail to have our clothes cleaned. Similarly, shoes should always be clean – especially the heels – as this shows attention to detail. I know of one senior manager who never ever recruits or promotes someone who has not polished his or her shoes prior to an interview. Your clothes say a great deal about you – make sure they say the right things.

But saying the right thing with the way you dress and the way you use your office will be wasted if your written and verbal communications fail to deliver the right image.

Your style of communication

We each have our own style in the way we communicate and we should not lose it; however, there are certain ground rules that, if followed, can improve the communication process, clarify the message (both for the sender and the receiver), and enhance our relationships with our colleagues and clients.

If we are to obtain the best performance from our team and to work well with our colleagues we need to be able to communicate our ideas and to have them understood. We all think we can communicate well, but communication is a two-way process and, although *we* may feel we have been clear, the other person may not have understood our message. As a high-ranking naval officer once remarked: 'I would like you to know that what you think you heard me say may not have been what I said nor what I meant to say.'

This remark is especially true when the language you are using as a means of communication with people is their second language, and even more so when it is your second language.

Much of the problem can be overcome if you are clear and unambiguous in what you say by steering clear of jargon. It also helps to keep your messages short and precise while, at the same time, saying what you need to say and not leaving anything out.

Written communication

The nature of today's business environment means that much of the communication with your team and with your management will have to be written. Memorandums recording instructions, reports conveying business results, and requests to other departments for assistance are all examples of when the written word is likely to convey the information in the clearest way.

Effective written communication means you need to THINK FIRST, THEN WRITE. Writing experts often say that clear writing is the result **of clear thinking**. Yet some people draft or dictate their letters right off the cuff – without stopping to think about the issues, the people involved, or the best course of action to suggest. If you are going to communicate effectively then you should use the three Ps – be Practical, Personal, and Positive, and you must adopt the most appropriate style.

The first step is to ensure you really know *what* you are to write about – to be **practical** and to get the facts. Ask yourself:

> 'What are the principal issues?'

The second step is know *who* you are going to write to – to be **personal** and try to determine your reader's feelings (if possible) from recent communications from them. Ask yourself:

> 'Who is my reader and what is in their mind?'

The third step is to be **positive** and decide that you are going to resolve the issue by carefully planning your communication based on your analysis of the issues (the facts) and your reader's profile (the feelings). Before you start to write you must ask yourself:

> 'How can I
>
> Respond? Resolve? Apologise? Thank?
>
> and Capitalize on the situation?'

The final step is to choose a **style**. Should you be assertive? Should you be objective? Should you be diplomatic? Or should you be informal? Obviously, elements of one style will overlap with another but you must be aware of the different styles, and choose deliberately.

Assertive An assertive communication gets right to the point. It's a good way to project your message with clarity and confidence. But save this style for instances when you have the upper hand. Otherwise, your forcefully worded statements may offend or discourage your reader.

When communicating in the assertive style:

- Use the active voice to give your message added punch. ('Please compile the reports and send them to me immediately', rather than 'The reports should be compiled as soon as possible')

- Say 'I' and 'You' to clarify who is responsible for what. ('I expect your answer on Monday' rather than 'We expect an answer on Monday')

- Say it directly ('Your report is overdue' rather than 'It has come to my attention that your report has not been received')

- Use simple sentences – avoid introductory phrases. ('I need your budget tomorrow' rather than 'Although time is short, I would appreciate your sending the budget to me tomorrow')

- Avoid 'weasel' words ('I'm confident this plan will work' rather than 'Perhaps this plan is the best alternative open to us').

Situations where this style is appropriate:

- when the communication calls for action
- when saying 'no' to a subordinate.

Objective Objective communications allow you to keep a polite distance between you and the reader. By design, they are impersonal in tone and a bit more formal than you normally write. Use this style when relaxed informality seems inappropriate or premature, or when an objective stance will make it easier to convey bad news without appearing accusatory. Objective communications remove your personality from a situation, so they should be reserved for instances where this is your intent.

When communicating in the objective style:

- Use the passive voice to distance yourself from negative situations or unpleasant observations. ('A more comprehensive plan should be supplied' rather than 'Expand the current plan before you send it')
- Emphasize the corporate 'we' – avoid saying 'I' or 'you' or using names. ('We believe that another financial obligation might cause undue strain' rather than 'I don't think you could handle a further loan, Mr Client')
- Maintain a formal tone by using polite words and phrases. ('In view of these reasons, I must decline the opportunity' rather than 'I just don't want the responsibility of another committee membership right now')
- Use certain 'slow-motion' techniques, like qualifiers, to delay the other person's confrontation with sensitive concepts. ('We cannot afford to extend you further credit under the circumstances' rather than 'I can't approve your loan').

Situations where this style is appropriate:

- when saying 'no' to a customer
- when responding to a simple inquiry from someone you don't know
- when conveying technical information to an audience
- when writing a routine memo to someone you don't know.

Diplomatic In certain delicate business situations, assuming a diplomatic attitude can help you demonstrate your respect for the other person. This tone signals that you are not out to prove yourself right, but rather to inform, clarify, or resolve situations to mutual satisfaction. Effectively used, this style positions you as being polite and can sometimes help the other person save face. But don't overdo it. If you are too humble or fawning, you will not be taken seriously.

When communicating in the diplomatic style:

- Use the passive voice to avoid placing the blame directly on others. ('The details were not available' rather than 'John Brown did not have the details available')

- Stress the corporate 'we', avoiding saying 'you' or 'I'. ('We're sorry to say' rather than 'I'm sorry to say')

- Offer suggestions instead of giving orders. ('Perhaps it would be wise to' rather than 'I recommend that you')

- Use introductory phrases and heavier paragraphs. ('Due to this unexpected problem, we' rather than 'I did not complete your transaction because')

- End on a positive or constructive note. ('We look forward to receiving your reply'.)

Situations where the diplomatic style is appropriate:

- in an internal communication to a person in a higher position

- in a communication conveying negative information.

Informal Communications in the informal style are relaxed, direct, and conversational. They acknowledge the personality of both parties; sometimes using elements like humour or colourful language that is inappropriate in most business communications. Your informal communications should reflect the way you speak. Keep them simple and sincere and they will be effective.

When communicating in the informal style:

- Use the active voice to show your personal involvement. ('We've credited your account' rather than 'Your payment was credited by us')
- Say 'I', 'we' and 'you'. ('I understand why you are angry' rather than 'Your anger is understandable')
- Use short words and sentences. ('Thanks for writing to me directly' rather than 'I certainly appreciate the fact that you directed this letter to my personal attention')
- Use contractions to sound conversational. ('**You're** right in your calculations, and **we'll** send your cheque today')
- Avoid 'weasel' words ('We will send the missing part with today's shipment' rather than 'It is possible that the missing part can be included in the shipment leaving today'.)

Situations where this style is appropriate:

- when apologising for an error
- when conveying good news
- when requesting action for a colleague at the same level as yourself
- when marketing a service or product
- when following up on a phone conversation.

Memorandums and Electronic mail

MEMORANDUM

To: All Managers
From: Alasdair White
Date: 21 July 1994
Subject: Writing Memos and Electronic Mail

As you know, memos and electronic mail are internal business communications used to convey information from one person or department to another. I'm writing this one to remind you of a few simple rules which can make your memos and electronic mail more effective.

1 Prepare to write your memos and electronic mail by using the three Ps. Be practical, be personal, then come up with a strategy for the memo or electronic-mail which will have a positive effect.

2 Match the style of the memo or electronic mail to the situation and to your relationship (junior, senior, peer) with the person to whom you are writing. Choose between the assertive, objective, diplomatic and informal styles.

3 Use a simple, easy-to-read format. Number your main points. Use 3.1, 3.2, etc., for sub-points. Indent or underline for emphasis.

4 Offer a choice of actions whenever possible.

5 Recap on the information that the reader needs to understand the issues raised in your memo or electronic mail, or attach relevant documents.

6 Keep memos and electronic mail to a reasonable length – generally no more than two pages.

In summary, effective memos and electronic mail follow the same basic rules as other effective business communications. They should be carefully conceived, clearly written, and presented in a format which makes important points easy to identify.

And finally, they should be proof read carefully for errors of content and grammar. Like any other piece of communication, your memos and electronic mail say a lot about you. Let it all be positive.

Communications checklist

Review the checklist below before communicating, especially in writing. It will help you become a more careful communicator – whether you have chosen the assertive, objective, diplomatic or informal style.

- Reply promptly. Communications are only as effective as they are timely.

- Use words correctly. Make sure you are using the correct words to convey your message. Make sure you have spelt them correctly.

- Use the language consistently. Ensure that you use either British English or American English but not a mixture of both. Check for spellings. Words sometimes have various meanings (e.g. 'year' can mean calendar year or financial year). Check that you have used words and specific terms to mean the same thing throughout your communication to avoid confusion.

- Avoid old-fashioned or stilted phrases. Phrases such as: 'in reference to', 'pursuant to', 'enclosed herewith', 'refer to the undersigned', 'your letter of the 14th inst', only make you sound pompous.

- Avoid jargon. Do not use in-house abbreviations which may be unclear to the reader.

- Be respectful. Even if you are saying no or pointing out an error. Remember, the client may not always be right but he is always the client; no one has ever won an argument with a client.

- Make sure your letter looks inviting. Make sure you have laid out your letter or memo in an attractive and easy-to-read way. Avoid large blocks of print by breaking up paragraphs or indenting to make points.

- Read your finished draft aloud. By reading the letter or

memo aloud you will see if it sounds natural and flows smoothly.

- Proof-read your letters and memos. Check for typing errors and grammatical errors.

- Edit your draft. If time allows, edit all written communications to cut out unnecessary words.

- Review your letters, memos, and electronic mail. Always read your written communications to see how they sound from the reader's point of view.

Spoken communication

I believe that more managers fail as leaders through bad spoken communication than through anything else. Inappropriate choice of words, inappropriate stress in a sentence, and a general lack of verbal skills will hold you back and can actively damage relationships with your colleagues, your boss, and your team. Let me be quite clear – I am not talking about your accent, although you should be aware that a heavy accent can take your listener some time to get used to; I am talking about spoken communication skills and much of what applies to written communication applies also to spoken communication.

Perhaps the most important spoken communication skill is not what you say but the way you **listen**. We have all come across managers who like the sound of their own voice and never let you say anything; and we have all tried to communicate with people who *hear* what you are saying but do not *listen*. Listening is a skill which can be learned and it is invaluable. There are two types of listening – **active** and **passive**.

Active listening requires a great deal of effort (which probably explains why so many people are bad at it) and concentration, and is part of a two-way process. As the speaker talks you should concentrate on their face and provide small signals that you have heard and understood – the occasional "Yes" or "Uh-hu" or even just a nod or shake of the head tells the speaker you are following what they are saying. Every so often you should stop the speaker and check important points to ensure you have understood – one friend of mine says, 'Let me see if I've understood that. What you're saying is' and then he repeats the key points that the speaker has made. This is especially important if the subject is complex because, if your understanding is not what the speaker wished you to understand, you have given him a chance to correct it. If you have got it correct then the speaker feels you are paying attention and can move on with the subject. Sometimes you may need to make notes – these should be brief and should be used to check back with the speaker at intervals.

Active listening is used when someone is imparting information on which you have to act – for example, a member of your team is presenting a problem and requires your advice. It is also used when you are trying to obtain information – you ask questions and then listen actively to the answer. In general terms, as a manager you will need to use active listening when dealing with your team, your colleagues, and your boss.

Passive listening is used when no response is required from you – for example, listening to presentations, listening to reports being delivered to a group (of course, when the report is being delivered to you, you have to use active listening). During passive listening you should watch the speaker (which tells him you are listening) but can make more copious notes for future reference.

The most important thing to remember is that listening is as much a visual activity as an audio activity – people who spend their time writing, doodling, staring out of the window, etc., are not listening, no matter what they might claim. Unfortunately, we hear much faster than we can speak and our brains want to get on with something else while the speaker is still trying to finish his sentence. For this reason, we should employ active listening principles whenever we can so that we remain focused on the message being delivered.

This is also important from the speaker's point of view since eye contact with the audience is the only sure way of knowing that they are listening.

Good listeners also make good communicators since they are in a position to ask the right questions and to supply the right responses.

Asking the right questions is also a skill. The purpose of questions is to obtain information and, as a manager, obtaining information from others is often vital to obtaining the performance you want from your team. Be warned, however, that questions should be open-ended (to obtain further information) rather than closed (requiring a yes/no answer). Only when you have obtained all useful information are you in a position to offer an appropriate response.

Now the roles are reversed. You, as the speaker, need to respond appropriately and that means thinking before you speak and choosing the right words. But good spoken communication goes beyond this: you also need to ensure what you are saying is being understood and I have found that one of the most effective methods of ensuring this is to apply the cliché 'It is not what you say but the way you say it'.

To be an interesting speaker, one that is easy to listen to, you need to vary the pitch of your voice, perhaps raising it to highlight a phrase or lowering it to draw the listener into the subject. You should also vary the pace of what you are saying and include some pauses. A faster pace shows enthusiasm while a slower speed focuses your listener's attention on your words rather than on you. Pauses are also very useful both to break up what is being said and to emphasise key phrases and ideas. People listen faster than you can speak and can often guess how you will end a sentence, pauses cause them to listen more slowly and to understand the message and provides a space for them to order their thoughts before you move on to the next idea.

Another useful trick is to use eye contact with the listener to emphasise a point but do not stare at them as this makes them uncomfortable and they will cease to listen effectively.

The making and breaking of eye contact while you are speaking involves your listeners – I am sure you have listened to people talking who never look at you when they speak and, like me, you have ceased to listen and have rapidly become bored.

Finally, remember to allow longer pauses so that your listeners can ask for clarification of anything you have said. This is very important if what you have to say contains a number of key ideas which build on each other. Stop after each point and ensure your listeners have understood.

Good speaking and listening skills can be learned. I have included some useful books on the subject in the Reading List and there is a growing number of companies offering communications skills training, but like all skills you need to practise what you have learned.

Personal objectives

The third area of personal development which is important for performance management is defining your personal objective. I am not talking about goals and objectives that are part of your job – what you have to achieve at work is very important but is not necessarily related to your personal objectives. Your personal objectives are what you want to achieve with your life, both at work and in your private life.

Goals in your working life

Business goals may include jobs you want to have tried, positions you want to have reached, responsibilities you want to have held and results you want to have delivered. In developing your personal business goals you will need to think carefully about what it is you want to achieve, decide on when you want to have achieved them, what you will have to do to reach your objectives (i.e. job moves, training courses, experience required) and then sit down and plan your career.

Whatever job you are doing now should be a step towards another objective along your career path and each step should be planned and a date set for its completion.

This exercise is not always as easy as it sounds and for many people it can be almost impossible – however, as a performance-orientated person, you really must take the time and make the effort. It is possible that your entire personal business goals can be achieved by a steady progression through your current company. On the other hand, in today's business world there are many, many opportunities around and you should realistically assess the alternatives. One computer programmer I knew decided that his personal business goals required him to set up on his own and he is now successfully running a very profitable company developing computer games. A senior manager in an oil company decided his personal business goals meant that he needed to move out of a business environment and into teaching at a business school. A friend of mine planned to stop working for the Ministry of Defence and become an artist – he gave himself until he was forty to achieve this objective and made the change by handing in his resignation on his fortieth birthday; he now supports himself and his family by painting, writing, and giving lectures on his work.

Of course, men are not the only ones who have goals in their working lives – more and more women are involved in business activities. One of my friends was faced with a difficult situation when her employer decided to move the department she worked in to another country – this acted as a catalyst and she chose to take redundancy and has now established her own very successful communications consultancy. Another woman I know worked for an oil company as an oil trader and, after some years, decided that she wanted to move into the strategic business planning. Her employer sponsored her to return to university to study for an MBA and she is now back with them working in the business planning department. And perhaps one of the most inspiring examples for me is that of a close friend I have known for over forty years who decided eighteen months ago that she wanted to run her own company – she is now the head of a small but extremely profitable nationwide organisation involving around twenty people, selling cosmetics and household products.

Taking your career in hand is vital if you are to progress – very few companies today plan the careers of their people and even fewer expect their employees to stay with them all their working lives. Peter Drucker, the management guru, talks of the modern worker being a 'knowledge worker' who takes his skills and knowledge to different jobs, often moving horizontally rather than seeking vertical promotion. This is particularly noticeable in the computer industry where spending five years with a company is the exception rather than the rule – where job changes (frequently to a different company) occur at intervals of eighteen months to two years. Far from being a bad thing, such movement rejuvenates companies with a constant inflow of new ideas and different perspectives. Most companies accept, and even welcome, the fact that good managers are managing their own careers and have definite plans as to what they should be doing next. The idea that you spend one year settling into a job, the second year doing the job, and the third year looking for and preparing to move to a new job is rather more common than most people believe.

Private goals

Beyond managing your career and achieving your business objectives, you should also have clear goals for your private life – again, with dates set for their achievement. Such goals could include getting married (or divorced!), buying a house, travelling in South America, or writing a novel. One woman announced that one of her goals was to trek to the Mount Everest base camp on her sixty-fifth birthday. A junior manager on one of my seminars announced that her goal was to sail round the world single-handed and then to learn to fly a helicopter, all by the time she was thirty-five – she completed the sailing trip at the age of thirty-four and flew her husband to a race meeting by helicopter just before she turned thirty-five.

Having distinct personal goals like this means you will always know where you are going and when you want to be there. Having a 'career' plan – both in business and personal areas – gives you the confidence to move forward and a person with confidence is a person others will follow. So self-confidence is a major contributor towards success in leadership.

SUMMARY POINTS:

- Whether or not you get to choose your team, you are still responsible for making sure you have the right people doing the right job.

- You are part of the team that has to achieve the objective.

- Questionnaires, when used to identify behaviours, are useful developmental tools.

- Managing your time well is vital to good performance.

- Be organised – always work on the most important thing to do right now.

- Use lists to help prioritise your work.

- Only have out on your desk those papers you need for the job you are doing right now.

- Delegate to others to ensure that you only do those things only you can do.

- Meetings should be well organised, they should have an agenda, and they should be worthwhile.

- Get the balance right between your responsibilities and between your work and private life.
- Your personal behaviour at work should always be professional and display calm self-confidence.
- Arrange and use your office to enhance performance rather than to reflect 'status'.
- In all your relations with your team, remember you are the leader and act accordingly.
- The way you dress should reflect the corporate image, any health and safety requirements, and the perceived preferences of the customers before reflecting your personal style.
- Your style of communication assists understanding – get the style right and communications will improve.
- Spoken communication uses the same styles as written communication.
- The most important spoken communications skill is *listening* and there are two types – *active* and *passive*.
- Manage your career – establish personal objectives, determine how you are going to achieve them, and make sure you are always working towards your goals.

4
Management Style – the Key to Success

Choosing the most effective management style • relationship orientation • your team's preferred management style • your own preferred management style • Personal Leadership Profile • Personal Behaviour Profile • managing foreign nationals • effective style – Performance Management at work

IN CHAPTER 1 we looked at the story of Steve Jones, a successful sales manager who was less than successful as a sales and marketing director because he had failed to realise that different people in different circumstances require different management styles. His personal style was inappropriate and he failed to adjust.

But what is management style and how can you decide what is your personal style? Over the years a great deal has been written about style and a variety of very interesting and useful books is available for those who have an academic interest. However, my approach is to focus on the practical, so I intend to discuss style in general and practical terms with the minimum of theory.

Choosing the Most Effective Management Style

In practical terms, the most effective management style is that which generates the best response from your team members – even if it is not your preferred style. The key here is that we have to manage people in the way *they* want or need to be managed rather than the way **we** want to manage.

Most of the style theories are based on two factors:

- relationship orientation, and
- task orientation.

Relationship orientation (RO)

This is the degree of personal interaction that is required. Some jobs require very little personal contact between the manager and the team member: for example, a financial control team generally prefers to be left alone to get on with the job and only wants to see the manager when it needs help. On the other hand, some jobs require a high degree of personal interaction for team members to 'bounce' ideas off the manager before proceeding: for example, a marketing department tends to work this way.

Task orientation (TO)

This is the degree of hands-on task focus that a manager needs to bring to the management of his team. Some jobs require a good deal of task management: for example, a production manager; while others require little task management: for example, managing a financial control team.

If relationship orientation and task orientation are taken together, then a style can be determined for a situation. To illustrate this, let us look at four people who may be under the control of one manager: a salesperson, a marketing officer, an administrative assistant, and a junior manager running a separate but dependent team.

The salesperson

Most salespeople require frequent contact with their manager for motivation purposes and for coaching of skills, but few need to be supervised closely and most are happy going about their job in a professional manner which may not bring them into contact with the manager more than once a day, if that. Clearly, this person does not need a high degree of RO from their manager.

On the other hand, managing a sales team requires the manager to be very high on TO – the manager needs to monitor performance, make sure goals are being achieved, that the team member is seeing enough customers, that orders are being properly logged and dispatched. And what is more, the team needs the manager to focus on the task.

In these circumstances, the manager needs to be high TO and medium RO in his approach:

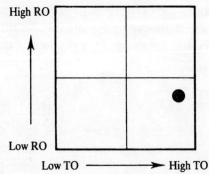

The black circle indicates the style needed to manage a member of the sales team

But what happens if the manager uses a high RO and medium TO style? I would suggest the likely outcome is that the sales team will consider that the manager is interfering and not letting them get on – this, in an extreme case, will result in irritation that eventually translates into demotivation. The other outcome is likely to be that the goals will not be achieved because the manager is not spending enough time on achieving the task.

The marketing officer

Most marketing professionals are highly creative individuals who, once the task has been defined, need very little 'managing' in terms of achieving the task. On the other hand, they need to spend a good deal of time 'brainstorming', discussing ideas, conceptualising, and seem to need frequent feedback of a positive nature.

In managing marketing people the manager needs to use a high RO and medium to low TO style:

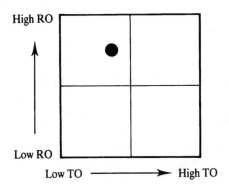

The black circle indicates the style needed with the marketing officer

So what is the likely outcome of using a low RO and high TO approach? Having seen this done, my experience is that rebellion sets in quickly, productivity declines, the marketing programmes deteriorate in quality, and the manager tends to have to do all the work himself.

The administrative assistant

The nature of an administrative assistant's work is that it is routine, with the same process being repeated over and over again. People working in this area become experts in the process and normally deliver a very high standard of work with few missed deadlines or mistakes. Because they are experts, and frequently know a great deal more about the process than the manager does, they are happy to be left completely alone to do their work. They require little contact with their manager or supervisor either in terms of the task or in terms of interpersonal relationship.

In managing administration people the manager needs to adopt a low RO and low TO style.

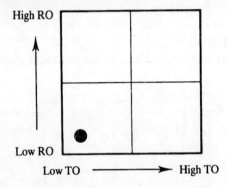

The black circle indicates the style needed with the administrative assistant

Any other style generally results in deterioration in the quality of the work, mistakes occur and are not rectified, the administrative assistant feels the manager does not trust him and demotivation sets in.

The junior manager
Junior managers running teams within a manager's department need to feel they are colleagues rather than subordinates. By the nature of their position they are obviously considered to be part of the 'management team' and feel valued when they can contribute to achieving the task (rather than carrying out orders). They like to be asked for their opinions and to participate in decision-making forums such as meetings.

In managing other managers the manager needs to adopt a high RO and high TO style:

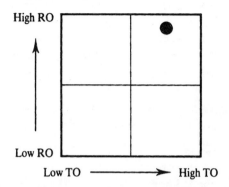

The black circle indicates the style needed with the junior manager

As with all inappropriate styles, the wrong style in this circumstance is likely to result in a decline in effectiveness and a deterioration in performance.

These four situations illustrate a need for four different styles of management to be used if the manager concerned is to be effective. They also illustrate that an inappropriate style will be less than effective and can lead to a serious deterioration in performance.

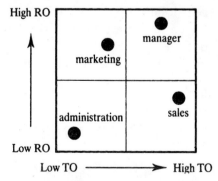

In this figure it is clear that the manager will have to adopt four different management styles in order to manage this team effectively.

YOUR TEAM'S PREFERRED MANAGEMENT STYLE

Your job as the manager is to select the most appropriate style to use in the management of the members of your team. To do this you need to ask yourself the following questions:

1 does the team member need me to be focused on the task and to keep him/her focused on the task – or is he task-orientated himself?

2 does the team member require a lot of contact with me so that she/he can do her job – or would she perform better if I kept out of the way?

At this point you must focus on what style they prefer you to use and must avoid falling into the trap of assuming that your preferred style is appropriate – it may be in certain circumstances but not in others. You must also remember that, unless all your team are doing the same job, you will need to use different styles with different people. This last point can be difficult especially when the same person carries out different roles within a team and will need to be managed differently in each situation.

You will also need to use a different style when managing people in groups for example, in a meeting – however, this is relatively easy since the subject of the meeting will tend to dictate the delivery and thus the style.

YOUR OWN PREFERRED MANAGEMENT STYLE

Your ability to be effective as a manager, to use different styles, depends on your understanding of those styles, your understanding of your own *preferred* management style, and of the interrelationship between them. Just as individuals prefer to be managed in certain ways, so you will prefer to manage in certain ways.

You should consider carefully the various combinations of RO and TO involved in choosing a style and decide on your strengths and weaknesses. For example, you may prefer focusing on the task and leaving your people to get on by themselves (high TO, low RO) or you may be the total opposite (high RO, low TO). Whichever style is your preferred style this is a strength but you will have to guard against its inappropriate use.

You should also decide on the style that you *least* like as this will be your weakness and you must guard against your avoiding it when it is appropriate. You may be fortunate and find that your preferred style is also the preferred style of your team – but remember the story of Steve Jones and act accordingly.

To understand your personal style you need to consider your preferences in terms of task orientation and relationship orientation and for this the work of Professor John Adair is useful. In his analysis of leadership he identified *Achieving the Task* (task orientation) as being a key action and he broke

The Adair model of leadership

relationship orientation into two – *Building the Team* and *Developing Individuals,* and then looked at how they were related. He perceived them as being three equally important actions and represented them as three interlinked circles as shown on the previous page.

The following questionnaire will enable you to see your current preferences and thus establish your preferred management style. High TO managers favour the top circle over the other two while high RO managers tend to have an underdeveloped TO and thus their top circle is considerably smaller than the other two. If all three of your circles are roughly equal then you have a very balanced style and will have the flexibility to change to suit the circumstances.

PERSONAL LEADERSHIP PROFILE

An assessment of the considerations and priorities which affect the leader's day-to-day activities

Instructions for completion

On the following pages, you will find thirty questions. Each question comprises a statement of a familiar management situation which is printed in bold type. This statement is followed by three different choices of management action. To complete each question, you must allocate five points between the three choices available. This allocation must be done in whole numbers, and the points which you allocate to each possibility should be placed in the box which is adjacent to that choice – as in the illustration on the facing page:

Management Style – The Key to Success

18 When you and your staff fail to meet an important deadline, do you:

i Identify the cause of the failure for future reference.

ii Let it pass, as it is now history and you have other jobs to be getting along with.

iii Assess each individual's performance in relation to the work achieved.

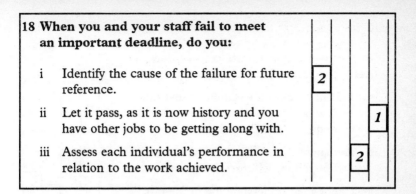

The allocation can, of course, vary between 5,0,0; 4,1,0; 3,1,1; or 2,2,1 – in any combination.

You will find that many of the management situations stated in bold type at the beginning of each question are familiar, and will remind you of actual things with which you have dealt in the past. When this is the case, you will find no difficulty in allocating the points according to your actual performance. When the management situations are not familiar to you, please allocate the points according to how you think you would actually perform in that sitaution.

All references to 'staff' and 'individuals' are intended to relate to those reporting *directly* to you with no intermediary.

When you have finished all the questions, you can add up the totals for each of the four columns on all pages of the questionnaire.

1 When individuals in your department are unhappy about a management decision, do you:

i Carry out the decision yourself, to set a personal example.

ii Call a meeting of your staff to discuss the problem.

iii Talk individually to those people who seem most unhappy.

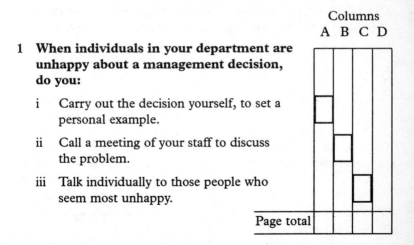

Managing for Performance

		Columns			
		A	B	C	D

2 **If members of your staff are not doing their jobs properly, do you**

    i   Inform them of the standards that must be met, and warn them of the consequences of not doing so.   [B]

    ii   Recognise it is a difficult time for them and hope they will sort themselves out.   [D]

    iii Check their understanding of the task and counsel them.   [C]

3 **When asked to achieve a task that you feel is not in your area of responsibility, do you:**

    i   Call a meeting with all staff in order to enlist their support.   [B]

    ii   Delegate it to someone who is usually willing to help.   [C]

    iii Get on with it and do it yourself.   [A]

4 **If an individual in your department is having difficulty getting their work done on time, do you:**

    i   Inform them of the standards that must be met, and warn them of the consequences of not doing so.   [B]

    ii   Ease their work load.   [D]

    iii Counsel them, and sort out any training needs.   [C]

Page total

Management Style – The Key to Success

                                             Columns
                                          A B C D

5 When discussing future targets with the boss, do you:

   i   Consider how well your team will achieve those targets. □(B)

   ii   Base future targets on past performance. □(A)

   iii Try to keep the targets low, to ensure a high level of achievement. □(D)

6 When you and your staff achieve an important and difficult deadline, do you:

   i   Call a meeting when all staff can discuss reasons for the success. □(B)

   ii   Compare the results carefully with the overall plan. □(A)

   iii Consider it part of the job and carry on with the next task. □(D)

7 If there is conflict amongst individuals in your team, do you:

   i   Hold a team meeting and try to resolve the conflict together. □(B)

   ii   Ensure everyone gets on with the job in order to take their minds off the conflict. □(A)

   iii Consider that these are the ups and downs of human relationships and they will sort themselves out in the long run. □(D)

Page total

	Columns			
	A	B	C	D

8 When you have set your staff a task, do you:

　i　Guide and encourage each person's performance. [C]

　ii　Inform them of the standards expected. [A]

　iii　Call a meeting and ask your team for their ideas. [B]

9 When informing your subordinates of a management decision, do you:

　i　Assemble your team and answer their questions. [B]

　ii　Consider carefully the involvement and development of each subordinate. [C]

　iii　Give each individual written instructions to ensure maximum accuracy. [A]

10 Before you decide on a course of action, do you:

　i　Base your decision on previous experience. [D]

　ii　Consider how each person in your team will be affected by the decision. [C]

　iii　Discuss with your team the best way to tackle it. [B]

Page total

Columns
A B C D

11 **When you delegate a task to a subordinate, to what extent do you:**

　i　Involve other members of your team in a discussion about the best way to tackle it.　[B]

　ii　Consider the ability and development of the person to whom you are delegating.　[C]

　iii　Ensure the individual completes the task according to the standards required.　[A]

12 **If one of your staff has difficulty completing their work on time, do you:**

　i　Counsel them and sort out their further training needs.　[C]

　ii　Inform them of the standards that must be met and warn them of the consequences of not doing so.　[A]

　iii　Involve the rest of the group in a discussion about the best way to overcome the problem.　[B]

13 **To ensure that the job is being done, do you:**

　i　Rely on one-to-one counselling for the best results.　[C]

　ii　Personally monitor the progress to make sure the correct standards are being achieved.　[A]

　iii　Obtain progress reports during staff meetings.　[B]

Page total

	Columns			
	A	B	C	D

14 Before agreeing to targets which are suggested for you and your team to achieve, do you:

i Consider the differing abilities of your team members to contribute to the targets. [C]

ii Work out a logical and mathematical approach to what you think those targets should be. [A]

iii Consult with your team on how it will cope with the proposed targets. [B]

15 When informing your subordinates of a management decision, do you:

i Put a memo on the bulletin board for all to see. [D]

ii Talk to everybody individually to ensure proper understanding. [C]

iii Call a team meeting to answer any questions. [B]

16 If there is a conflict amongst individuals in your team, do you:

i Consider that these are the ups-and-downs of human relationships and they will sort themselves out in the long run. [D]

ii Speak to those individuals involved and try to sort out the problem. [C]

iii Hold a team meeting and try to resolve the problem together. [B]

Page total

	Columns			
	A	B	C	D

17 When you discipline a member of staff, do you:

   i   Inform them of the standards that must be met and the consequences of failing to do so.

   ii   Hold a team meeting to try to resolve the problem together.

   iii   Counsel the individual concerned and encourage them to agree standards for the future.

18 When you and your staff fail to meet an important deadline, do you:

   i   Identify the cause of the failure for future reference.

   ii   Let it pass, as it is now history and you have other jobs to be getting along with.

   iii   Assess each individual's performance in relation to the work achieved.

19 When someone has done work for you incorrectly, do you:

   i   Correct it yourself and tell them where they have gone wrong.

   ii   Correct it yourself but don't say anything.

   iii   Explain why the work was incorrect and encourage them to alter it to meet your needs.

Page total

Columns
A B C D

20 If you are not happy with the working condidtions for you and your staff, do you:

i Consult individually with your subordinates to find out their points of view. [C]

ii Speak to your senior management in order to sort things out. [A]

iii Involve your staff in a group discussion on the best way to tackle the problem. [B]

21 When a new person joins your department, do you:

i Ensure they understand the standards and targets they must achieve. [A]

ii Introduce them to everybody at a team meeting. [B]

iii Counsel them on how best they can contribute to the overall plan. [C]

22 When ensuring that work is being carried out satisfactorily, are you more likely to:

i Personally monitor progress to make sure correct standards are being achieved. [A]

ii Ask for progress reports during staff meetings. [B]

iii Rely on one-to-one counselling to produce the best overall result. [C]

Page total

Columns
A B C D

23 When it comes to making a decision, do you prefer to:

i Rely on previous experience so that there is less chance for error. [D]

ii Consider carefully how each individual will be affected by the decision. [C]

iii Call a meeting to obtain ideas from the group. [B]

24 When communicating with your staff on a daily basis, do you:

i Hold informal departmental meetings to ensure that everyone is aware of the total situation. [B]

ii Consider the involvement and development of each member of your staff. [C]

iii Ensure everyone understands the quality and standards required for the job in hand. [A]

25 When you and your staff fail to meet an important deadline, do you:

i Call a meeting of all your staff to discuss where things went wrong. [B]

ii Assess each individual's performance in relation to the work achieved. [C]

iii Identify the cause of the failure for future reference. [A]

Page total

Columns
A B C D

26 When it comes to making a decision, do you prefer to:

　i　Call a meeting to obtain ideas from the group. [B]

　ii　Consider carefully your resources and constraints. [A]

　iii　Rely on previous experience as you feel that there is then less chance for error. [D]

27 When individuals in your department are unhappy about a management decision, do you:

　i　Carry out that decision yourself, to set a personal example. [A]

　ii　Ensure that union/staff representatives are well informed to answer questions. [D]

　iii　Counsel those individuals who seem most unhappy. [C]

28 When dealing with normal routine matters during the day, do you:

　i　Hold informal meetings with the staff to ensure everyone is in touch with the total situation. [B]

　ii　Ensure that the quality and quantity of the work is maintained to a high standard. [A]

　iii　Consider that the day-to-day matters have their ups and downs and are unimportant compared to the finished job. [D]

Page total

29 **Before agreeing to targets which are suggested for you and your team to achieve, do you:**

   i Try to keep your targets low, to ensure a high level of achievement.

   ii Consider the differing abilities of your staff to contribute to the overall objectives.

   iii Discuss with your team their ideas in order to help improve your understanding.

30 **When informing your subordinates about a management decision, do you:**

   i Issue everyone with written instructions to ensure maximum accuracy.

   ii Assemble your team and answer their questions.

   iii Consider the involvement and development of each individual in your team.

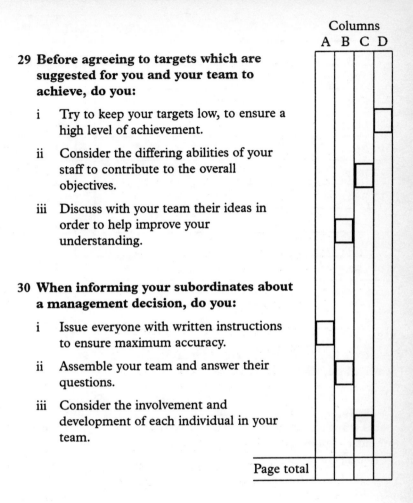

Scoring instructions:

To produce a total score for this questionnaire, you must first add up the totals from all five pages. This can be done on the chart on the next page.

Now you have heard about Dr John Adair's Functional Leadership Model, you should know that your total scores represent the respective consideration which you give to each of the circles which comprise the model.

	A	B	C	D
1st page				
2nd page				
3rd page				
4th page				
5th page				
6th page				
7th page				
8th page				
9th page				
10th page				
11th page				
Grand total				

A score is the **Task**, **B** score is the **Team** and **C** score is the **Individual**,

Taking the **A** score, you can start filling in the **Task** circle. The 'bullseye' represents ten points, and each circle thereafter represents a further ten points. Shade in the **Task** circle with the correct number of points.

Repeat the exercise for both the **Team** and the **Individual** circles. You now have a graphic picture of your preferred leadership functions – and more importantly the function(s) which you do not consider enough.

The **D** scores throughout the questionnaire represent a preference for 'non-management' action. Although it is technically possible to score seventy-five points for the **D** score, the 'ideal' score should be less than ten points. fifteen points suggests that thee options were consistently considered – although usually rejected. Any score in excess of fifteen suggests that these options are always considered and the higher the score, the more frequently they are used.

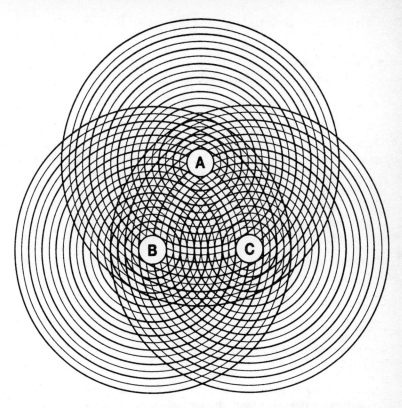

Some notes about the Functional Leadership Model

Effective leadership derives from the leader always considering three fundamental elements when taking any action. These are the needs to:

1. Achieve the task

This need is not only important for its own sake, but on its fulfilment will hang the morale of the group and the degree to which each person in the group shares the sense of achievement which results.

2. Develop individuals

Each person in the group has a need to develop and to satisfy a wide range of motivational needs. These include the needs to achieve and grow, as well as the social and belonging needs.

3. Build a team

The effect of high team spirit derives from a real community of purpose. Such a team produces synergy – a high level of task achievement – and a morale which is supportive of its own members.

It immediately becomes clear that these three fundamental areas of leadership are interdependent. Insufficient consideration of any area will have an adverse effect on the other areas, i.e.:

1. Failure to achieve the task produces low morale. This soon degenerates into individuals concentrating on their 'own' interests.

2. Low team spirit produces an environment where there is no synergy. Where, rather than helpful cooperation, there is hostile competition. Clearly this atmosphere will have an adverse effect on the achievement of the task.

3. Failure to develop an individual will result in that person being a potential demoralising influence within the team. This will obviously distract the team from the achievement of the task.

In order to illustrate this critical interdependence of the three areas Dr John Adair produced the following Model:

The three interlocking and overlapping circles clearly demonstrate the essential need for the leader to ALWAYS consider ALL the areas before taking any action at all

Guidelines for interpreting your scores

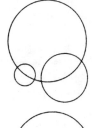

Task-centred approach – allied to a recognition that individuals have a contribution to make.

DANGER! There is a touch of 'divide and rule' about this score. The morale is probably a lot worse than you think and too much energy is going into other things apart from the task.

Task-centred approach – allied to a recognition that the staff do need to know what is going on.

DANGER! Your staff probably see you as riding roughshod over them. This will certainly affect their commitment to the task, and in the long term could produce active resistance to it.

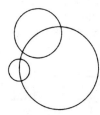

Individual-centred approach – allied to an acceptance that the task has to be achieved.

DANGER! Your concern for team-building is too low and could produce petty jealousies between individuals who will see you as having favourites (however unfairly).

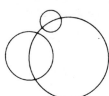

Individual-centred approach – allied to a recognition that those individuals have a need to get on well together.

DANGER! Your lack of concern for the task is limiting the REAL development of your people in such areas as their needs for challenge and achievement. They are likely to leave and go somewhere where these needs can be fulfilled.

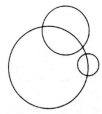

Team-centred approach – allied to a recognition that loss of task achievement would adversely affect team spirit.

DANGER! You are apt to expect everyone to suborn his individual needs to those of the team. You are too anxious to be 'one-of-the-boys'.

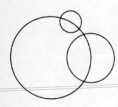

Team-centred approach – allied to a concern for the needs of individuals. A very 'people-centred' profile suggesting that you see the group as a club.

DANGER! Even the best clubs have a purpose to their existence. If the purpose is not fulfilled there is an adverse effect on morale which results in individuals changing clubs.

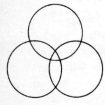

The ideal profile. This shows an equal concern for each of the leadership areas. The result should be a high level of task achievement, high morale and considerable commitment from all concerned.

Reproduced with permission from Sandy Ellvers-Dix

In every management role there will be times when what you want your people to do will be different from what they want to do. This situation causes conflict which needs to be resolved – you may choose to order obedience or to request compliance, you may seek a compromise or you may avoid the issue – whatever approach you use is part of your management style. If you are to get the best performance from your team you need to understand your preferred style of handling conflict and to recognise that there is no right or wrong approach but simply an appropriate or inappropriate response to the situation.

The following questionnaire is designed to assess your preferred behaviour in response to situations involving conflict. Again, there are no right or wrong answers and the results show your normal responses in terms of four key behaviours – *Assertive, Aggressive, Accommodating,* and *Avoidance*.

Personal Behaviour Profile

An assessment of the considerations and priorities which affect an individual's behaviour

Instructions for completion

On the following pages you will find thirty questions. Each question comprises a statement of a familiar situation which is printed in bold type. This statement is followed by three different choices of action. To complete each question you must allocate five points between the three choices available. This allocation must be done in whole numbers, and the points which you allocate to each possibility should be placed in the box which is adjacent to that choice – as in the illustration below:

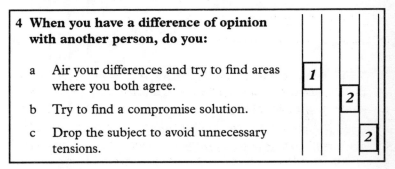

The allocation can, of course, vary between 5,0,0; 4,1,0; 3,1,1; or 2,2,1 – in any combination.

You will find that many of the situations stated in bold type at the beginning of each question are familiar, and will remind you of actual things which you have experienced in the past. When this is the case, you will find no difficulty in allocating the points according to your actual behaviour. When the situations are not familiar to you, please allocate the points according to how you think you would actually behave in that situation.

When you have finished all the questions, you can add up the totals for each of the four columns on all pages of the questionnaire.

	Columns
	A B C D

1 **When working with others on trying to solve a problem, do you usually:**
   a Try to work together to sort out a solution.
   b Try to be firm in pursuing your ideas.
   c Just let the others get on with it.

2 **When you are trying to get on with work and someone interrupts you, do you:**
   a Explain why you're busy and arrange to contact them later.
   b Stop what you're doing and listen to them so you don't offend them.
   c Tell them you are too busy to talk to them.

3 **When you are having an important discussion with one other person and your phone rings, do you:**
   a Carry on with the call and deal with it straightaway in order to get it out of the way.
   b Check the priority of the call and accordingly defer it or explain to the person you are with why you must deal with it.
   c Deal with the call but apologise profusely to the person you are with.

Page total

Columns
A B C D

4 **When you have a difference of opinion with another person, do you:**

   a Air your differences and try to find areas where you both agree.

   b Try to find a compromise solution.

   c Drop the subject to avoid unnecessary tensions.

5 **When you are asked by a superior to do extra work which you don't think you have time for, do you:**

   a Accept the work and hope you will be able to fit it in.

   b Explain your problems factually showing that if the extra work is to be done then you will have to drop some other work.

   c Accept the work but say at the time you are worried about your time available.

6 **When someone has done work for you incorrectly, do you:**

   a Correct it yourself and tell them where they have gone wrong.

   b Explain why the work was incorrect and encourage them to alter it to meet your needs.

   c Correct it yourself but don't say anything.

Page total

Columns
A B C D

7 When you feel that someone's behaviour towards you is unfair, do you:

a Tell them what is wrong with their behaviour and what they should do about it. — B

b Cover up the feelings you have about their behaviour in order to preserve the relationship. — D

c Calmly discuss your feelings about their behaviour and try to reach a mutual solution. — A

8 Would you say about yourself in relationships that you try to:

a Consider the other person's wishes and feelings. — C

b Tell people what you feel and believe, although it may hurt their feelings. — B

c Be open-minded and look for common ground. — A

9 When someone criticises something you have done, do you:

a Accept there may be truth in the criticism and try to air one another's points of view. — A

b Retaliate by pointing out a mistake they have made. — B

c Accept the criticism. — C

Page total

Columns
A B C D

10 When the majority of members at a meeting oppose your views, do you:

   a Retire from the discussion as it is not worth the effort.

   b Try to win your position.

   c Sacrifice your wishes for those of others.

11 When someone wants to borrow something that you are not keen on lending, do you:

   a Say 'yes' reluctantly to avoid unnecessary tension.

   b Just flatly say 'no'.

   c Explain calmly and factually why you are not keen to lend it.

12 When you want someone to do some work for you but you know they are busy, do you:

   a Explain that you understand they are busy, but try to work out together how to get your needs met.

   b Ask them to do it when they have the time.

   c Try to be firm in pursuing your goals.

Page total

13 **When you know someone has said unfair things about you behind your back, do you:**

   a Have a show-down with them and tell them their faults.

   b Carry on as if nothing has happened.

   c Attempt to get all concerns and issues out into the open in a calm manner.

14 **When you have a dispute with someone and have stated your views honestly but firmly, afterwards do you feel:**

   a That it was good to appreciate each other's point of view.

   b That you were right and they were wrong and making your point was important.

   c A little guilty for having been so firm.

15 **When reviewing work done with others which has failed to meet its objectives, do you:**

   a Say no one's really at fault as we were all working together.

   b Point out where everyone has gone wrong.

   c Regard the results as water under the bridge and get on with the next task.

	A	B	C	D
13a		✓		
13b			✓	
13c	✓			
14a	✓			
14b		✓		
14c			✓	
15a			✓	
15b		✓		
15c				✓
Page total				

Management Style – The Key to Success

Columns
A B C D

16 When someone proudly shows you something that you don't really like, do you:

a Tell them you don't like it because you feel you must be honest. [B]

b Say that you like it because you don't want to hurt their feelings. [C]

c Appear interested but quickly change the subject. [D]

17 When you have to give somebody some disappointing news, do you:

a Tell them short and sharp as facts have to be faced. [B]

b Tell them but try to soothe their feelings to preserve the relationship. [C]

c Break the news but at the same time tell them that you understand their disappointment and try to work together for a positive outcome. [A]

18 When you need to talk to someone urgently but they are in deep conversation with another person, do you:

a Wait until they have finished talking. [D]

b Apoligise for interrupting and ask for a moment of their time. [C]

c Acknowledge that you are interrupting but calmly explain your needs factually. [A]

Page total

	Columns			
	A	B	C	D

19 Would you say about yourself in relationships that you try to:

   a Consider the other person's wishes and feelings. — C

   b Have an open discussion so that you can look for points of agreement. — A

   c Do what is needed to avoid unnecessary tension. — D

20 When you have a difference of opinion with another person, do you:

   a Air your differences and try to find areas where you both agree. — A

   b Try to show them the logic and benefits of your position. — B

   c Try to consider their wishes in reaching a solution. — C

21 When someone has successfully completed work for you, do you:

   a Just say 'Well done' because you don't want to go on about it as it is water under the bridge. — B

   b Thank them and tell them how grateful you are. — C

   c Say 'Well done' and why you think it's successful. — A

Page total

Management Style – The Key to Success

Columns
A B C D

22 When someone keeps interrupting you when you are trying to make a point, do you:

a Tell them that if they were at all reasonable they wouldn't interrupt.

b Acknowledge their input is important to them, but calmly inform them you would like to finish making your point.

c Ask them nicely if they would mind not interrupting you.

23 After having disagreements with others do you normally feel:

a You have to convince them of the logic and benefits of your position.

b You have to find a compromise solution.

c That differences are not always worth worrying about.

24 When working with others in trying to solve a problem, do you:

a Try to work together to reach a solution.

b Try to ensure everyone is happy with the solution.

c Try to be firm in pursuing your ideas.

Page total

Managing for Performance

	Columns			
	A	B	C	D

25 In general when dealing with others, do you:

a Like to assert your wishes. — B

b Sometimes sacrifice your own wishes for the wishes of others. — C

c Like to get all concerns and issues out in the open. — A

26 If the actions of an individual upset the rest of the group, do you:

a Usually ignore it as it may aggravate the situation and will probably be sorted out by the rest of the group. — C

b Tell them what they are doing wrong. — B

c Tell them your views based on fact and state what effect their actions have on the group. — A

27 When an individual has a different point of view which opposes yours, do you:

a Explore their arguments to get understanding and look for areas of agreement. — A

b Try to meet their wishes by shifting your position. — C

c Do what is necessary to avoid tension. — D

Page total

Columns
A B C D

28 If someone is not doing a job for you the way you want it, do you:

   a Point out what they are doing wrong and how they should correct it.

   b Explain why you are not satisfied and work out jointly a course of actions to meet your needs.

   c Accept that errors will happen and hope the individual will learn from their mistake.

29 When you have to give somebody some disappointing news, do you:

   a Break the news but try to soothe their feelings to preserve the relationship.

   b Try to postpone the issue until you have had some time to think it over.

   c Break it to them short and sharp as there is no point dragging things out.

30 When you have to fill in personality questionnaires such as this one, do you:

   a Fill it in because you have been asked to.

   b Feel that something positive can be gained from the experience.

   c Think all questionnaires are time-wasters.

Page total

Scoring instructions:

To produce a total score for this questionnaire, you must first add up the totals from all pages. This can be done on the chart below.

	A	B	C	D
1st page				
2nd page				
3rd page				
4th page				
5th page				
6th page				
7th page				
8th page				
9th page				
10th page				
Grand total				

Now that you have had the four 'As of the behaviour continuum explained to you, you should now know that your total scores represent the respective tendencies you have for each of the four areas.

A score is **Assertive** behaviour
B score is **Aggressive** behaviour
C score is **Accommodating** behaviour
D score is **Avoiding** behaviour

Taking your four scores, you can now plot your Personal Behavioural Profile Graph.

Management Style – The Key to Success

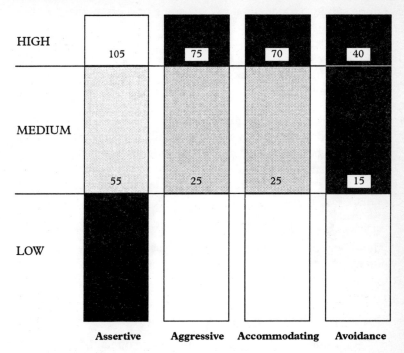

The scoring system has been standardised after four years' research by LPT Productions.

Behaviour definitions

Assertive behaviour
Standing up for your personal rights and expressing thoughts, feelings and beliefs in DIRECT, HONEST and APPROPRIATE ways which do not violate another person's rights. It enables you and others to keep your self-esteem and should lead to a better understanding without damaging relationships. Respect is shown for the rights of others, not deference, appeasement, apology or self-effacement which are non-assertive behaviours.

Aggressive behaviour
Even though this behaviour is competitive and is usually concerned with results, it often offends and violates another person's rights. It

can be subtle and done in a well-meaning or pleasant manner, but it expresses itself in a way that will invade another person's (physical/psychological) space.

Aggressive behaviour can occur as a result of a build-up of 'straws that break the camel's back' or when one has doubts about one's ability to control a situation.

Accommodating behaviour
Expressing your views, thoughts and feelings in such a way that they can be disregarded, misconstrued so that others may take advantage of you. It is not honest and usually has avoidance of conflict as its goal. It relies on others being responsible and not violating your rights.

Avoidance behaviour
Ignores any violation of your own rights, usually for fear of the reaction of others. It consists of evading any honest confrontation, often by flight.

Guidelines for interpreting your scores

☐ High Assertive
   with
☐ Low Aggressive
☐ Low Accommodating
☐ Low Avoidance

You try to be direct, honest and appropriate in your behaviour. You show respect for the rights of others and you are able to use Assertive techniques to collaborate with others in finding mutual solutions.

☐ High Assertive
   with
▨ Medium/High Aggressive
▨ Medium/High Accommodating

You are aware of Assertive techniques, but you may not be able to pick the right behaviour to suit situations. This can be achieved through controlled conscious effort.

Management Style – The Key to Success

■ High Aggressive — You have a competitive spirit but you may achieve your goals at the expense of others.

DANGER: AGGRESSIVE BEHAVIOUR GENERALLY LEADS TO OTHERS FEELING RESENTMENT TOWARDS YOU.

■ High Aggressive
with
▨ Medium Assertiveness
▨ Medium Accommodation

Your Assertive techniques are manipulative and you may spend a lot of time repairing hurt feelings.

■ High Aggressive
with
■ High Accommodating
■ High Avoidance

You are tolerant to a point, but the only response you use when you want to stand up for your rights is Aggression.

■ High Aggressive
with
☐ Low Accommodating
☐ Medium Assertive

You try to honestly speak your mind, but you may come across as too pushy and critical.

■ High Accommodating — This approach has harmony and the avoidance of 'needless' unpleasantness as its goal. It works well if everybody is sensitive to each other and respects each other's rights.

DANGER: YOU WILL EVENTUALLY FEEL GREAT FRUSTRATION IF YOU ARE NOT GETTING YOUR NEEDS MET AND YOUR BEHAVIOUR WILL EVENTUALLY TURN TO AGGRESSION OR COMPLETE WITHDRAWAL.

■ High Accommodating
　with
■ High Avoidance

You have many issues which you have difficulty dealing with. Problems will be minimised or shuffled around but not solved.

■ High Accommodating
　with
■ High Aggressive

You tend to let problems build up until a breaking point is reached instead of trying to solve them at the first sign of trouble.

★ ★ ★ ★ ★ ★ ★

■ High Avoidance

This behaviour is concerned with ignoring people's behaviour. Like Accommodation, it minimizes conflict and your reaction is to back down at the first sign of competitiveness.

DANGER: THIS BEHAVIOUR OFTEN ENCOURAGES OTHERS TO BE AGGRESSIVE TOWARDS YOU AND INVADE YOUR SPACE.

■ High Avoidance
　with
■ High Aggressive
▢ High Assertive

Have you based your answers on how you would like to be perceived rather than on how you actually behave?

Although it is technically possible to score sixty-five points for the Avoidance score, the ideal score should be less than fifteen. More than fifteen points indicates that immediate attention should be given to overcoming Avoidance behaviour. Please do not ignore this warning if you wish to succeed in life.

Reproduced with permission from Sandy Ellvers-Dix

For further information on style I recommend the work of Professor John Adair, Professor William Reddin, and the books by Kenneth Blanchard – I have listed their books in the Reading List.

MANAGING FOREIGN NATIONALS

As we get further into the 1990s, more and more managers are finding themselves faced with running teams made up of different nationalities or even teams based in countries other than their own. This situation can and does present a number of additional problems.

Not only do you have to be aware of the personal style but also that different nationalities have different cultural characteristics and will view your style in different ways. They may also have different preferred styles of management and of being managed. You may even have to contend with the fact that your team members do not speak the same language as you do – that one of you will have to work in a second or even third foreign language, with all that that implies in terms of understanding and cultural impact.

Research carried out by Ashridge Management College in the United Kingdom in 1993 into pan-European management gave rise to the conclusion that international management was more than a matter of doing the same things in a different country. Language and national cultural characteristics impacted on the way the role of the manager is viewed, and, therefore, the way the manager's actions are viewed. What could be normal management practice in one country could be unusual or even unacceptable in another.

The Ashridge research also suggests that in some cultures, such as in the UK and USA, there is a perception that management and leadership are two different, although related, activities; while in other cultures there is no such distinction – in fact, in many western European countries such a distinction is rejected totally and management and leadership are not even seen as two sides of the same coin – they are considered one and the same thing.

My own research (based on observation and thus less empirical than that of Ashridge) suggests that too great an emphasis is placed on the difference perceived. My experience in teaching performance management techniques throughout Europe, the Middle East and Asia has shown me that the skills and concepts are universal but that delivery is affected by the culture. My experience is that goals, goal setting, performance monitoring, performance reviews, appraisals, and so on, are easily accepted at all levels but the way they are established and delivered changes according to the country in which they are being operated.

An example of this cultural impact can be found in the attitude towards individual performance goals. In those countries with a very strong 'social democratic' political environment, such as Germany, Belgium, and Spain (to name just three), there is a very strong **union** influence and this impacts on the way the 'workers' view individual performance goals. In some countries, Germany for example, it has proven to be very difficult to convince the unions that individual goals do not threaten the worker's job. In fact, such is the resistance from the unions that companies wishing to motivate their people through individual goals have faced strike action.

Where management has been successful in gaining cooperation from the unions over individual goals, the performance of the people has improved dramatically, staff turnover has dropped, profits have risen, and salaries have gone up. This, I believe, supports the concept that if you give people a clear objective they will strive to achieve it.

But can it be argued that these difficult attitudes towards individual goals stems from 'cultural' or 'national' characteristics? They do, to a certain extent, but I believe they also stem from the political environment and can also be found in the UK and USA in highly unionised companies.

The Adair view of leadership – that it is what the leader

does that is important and not what the leader is – focuses on the three action areas: achieving the task, building the team, and developing the individual, and these areas remain critical in all the cultures and countries I have encountered. What does change, however, is the way the leader or performance manager delivers each of these action areas. And this can be impacted by the structural make-up of the organisation and it corporate culture — something that is frequently a reflection of national characteristics.

A good example of this would be a US company operating with a European division. In such a company the corporate culture will reflect the US background of the parent rather than the European background of the local division. This becomes rather more complicated when the US company grows by acquiring existing European companies and turning them into subsidiaries – in this case, the corporate culture of the subsidiary will reflect its national characteristics rather than those of the parent company and 'head office' managers may well have considerable problems managing the local business. To overcome this, the parent company will have to 'manage differently' or undertake a lengthy and uncertain process of cultural change.

Corporate culture, however, is not the same as national culture – although it may reflect it. There is good evidence that when people join a company with a corporate culture that does not reflect their national cultural characteristics they are no less successful – **provided they understand and accept the corporate culture** and work within it. Thus there are plenty of examples of Germans working in US companies and being successful; of French working for British companies, of Greeks working for Arab companies, and so on.

The key is to deliver performance management techniques within the corporate culture while being aware that national characteristics will have an effect on the way things are understood. To ignore the national characteristics of the team is to court danger; however, they are but one of the aspects which you will need to consider when establishing the most appropriate management style to use.

A much greater hindrance to good performance management is an overly politicised corporate culture or one that is heavily influenced by the unionised thinking of the last forty years. In such an environment you may find your efforts to establish performance management techniques are met with suspicion and possibly outright hostility. As with any such situation where change is desirable, change is also feared, and you would be wise to take things slowly. You will need to build your credibility with your team, build the team to achieve the task, and let success in these areas support the introduction of ideas that will allow the development of the individual. After all, no manager would just suddenly introduce a new way of managing – he would always bring things in by stages to obtain acceptance, and the irreversibility, of the change.

SUMMARY POINTS

- Management style (as opposed to management techniques) is based on the relationship between relationship orientation (RO) and task orientation (TO).

- There are four basic types of style: low RO, low TO; high RO, low TO; low RO, high TO; high RO, high TO.

- The most effective management style is that which generates the best response from the team member.

- Different team members doing different jobs require different management styles – to be effective you need to choose the right style for the person to be managed.

- Management style also includes how you deal with conflict.

- The wrong choice of style causes deterioration in performance.

- Your job is to select the right style to use with each person.

- As the manager, you will have a preferred style and a style you do not like using – these are your strong and weak styles and they should not be over- or under-used, but used appropriately.

- The combination of the right management style with the skills and techniques discussed throughout this book will produce the most effective management for your team.

- Different national characteristics and languages cause people to view management styles differently.

- Although leadership and the role of the manager are viewed in different ways in different countries, the core skills and concepts of performance management are universal.

- The delivery of the core skills is affected by national characteristics.

- The political and union environments have greater impact on the acceptance of performance management techniques than do national characteristics.

- The corporate culture also affects the way in which the performance management techniques are perceived.

- A good performance manager takes into account corporate culture and national characteristics when selecting the most appropriate management style.

5

People – the Human Resource

The Job Specification • performance standards • the Job Profile • Staff Characteristics Profile • obtaining the resource • recruiting • reassigning • confirming an existing assignment • ensuring the person has the right knowledge • implementing Job Specifications • annual appraisals • forced ranking

IT IS PROBABLY TRUE for most managers that they seldom have the chance to choose their own team – people are, on the whole, either inherited when taking over the job, or they are assigned to the team with little in the way of input from the manager. It is very rare for a manager to be able to select his entire team or to be able to change the team members to reflect changing objectives. Unfortunately, it is also rare for a manager to have any real influence over the selection procedure when filling gaps in his team.

And yet almost everyone will claim that, in their organisation, people are considered to be the most important resource.

It is also true that many people make the almost inevitable mistake of choosing team members on the basis of whether they like them or not, rather than whether the person is the right one to fill the role that has to be undertaken. It is also true that most managers will shy away from selecting people who **are not like them and do not think like them** and yet this approach often results in a bland, conformist, subservient grouping rather than a dynamic, creative and motivated team. For this reason, a great many companies choose to place the responsibility for recruitment and selection firmly in the hands of the Human Resources department who are supposed to be experts in this field.

But there is a danger here as well: if you have no influence over the selection process then the allocation or assignment of the (human) resource is not likely to match your requirements. It is imperative, therefore, that you should play an active role in the selection of your team so that you have the best resources for achieving the objectives you have been given.

To avoid a mismatch of resources you need to have a very clear idea of what resources you need and this is especially true of your team. The first step, therefore, is to develop – for each job in the team – a specification of the job to be done and a 'profile' of the type of person needed in the role. Then match your current people against the specification and profile to ensure they fit – if they do not, a decision has to be made as to whether training can ensure a fit or the person needs to be replaced or reassigned. This is a tough call but remains a primary responsibility for you if you are to achieve your objectives.

So how do you develop a job specification and profile?

THE JOB SPECIFICATION

The Job Specification is a factual description of what the objective of the job is and what has to be done to reach it. It clearly defines *all* the primary responsibilities and generally includes the secondary responsibilities which are frequently expressed in loose, subjective terms such as 'working well with other team members'. It also defines the immediate working sub-group, the position's reporting line – both upwards and downwards, i.e. who the position reports to and who reports to the position, and where the job is positioned in terms of the corporate structure.

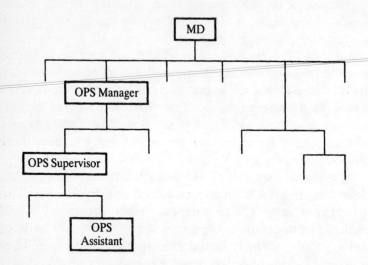

An example of an organisational diagram for a job specification for an Operations Assistant

This document is not meant to be restrictive and you should certainly make it flexible; however, you must clearly define what is an acceptable **level of performance** in each area of responsibility.

The first step in development of a job specification is to analyse the role in terms of achieving the job objective. What has to be done, when it has to be done, and what is the minimum standard of performance required in doing it. This process of analysing what has to be done, and when, is usually two-way, between you and the job-holder (if it is an existing job) or between you and the HR department (if it is a new job). The job should be separated into all its constituent parts, reviewed for accuracy and completeness, and the responsibilities written down. This should result in an accurate and realistic description of the job.

You should also view the job in terms of the overall objective of the team – asking yourself: Is this job necessary for the achievement of the team goals?

But what of the performance standard expected?

Performance standards

Many corporations confuse **goals** with **performance standards** (norms or benchmarks) and this leads to conflict when annual performance appraisals are carried out. The performance standards define the minimum performance acceptable in that job and are used to determine training requirements and whether the job functions and responsibilities have been carried out satisfactorily – in fact, whether the person is performing in accordance with the specifications. (In much the same way that you would expect a piece of machinery to perform in accordance with the specifications.) Goals are always higher than the minimum performance standards and are designed to elicit a higher performance.

If we were to take a hard look at this, it would be fair to say that a person failing to meet minimum performance standards (MPSs) either is in urgent need of training or should not be in that job. Whereas a person who fails to achieve their goals is more likely to be suffering a lack of motivation. Conversely, a person who reaches the MPS has earned the right to the job and a person who has achieved his goals (or exceeded them) has earned more than his salary and should be given recognition and, possibly, a bonus.

Goals are such an important subject in themselves that they are covered in a chapter of their own, Chapter 9.

So how do we establish the minimum performance standards (MPS) for each job?

There are three sources of help:

- internal benchmarks – what are other people doing in similar functions within the business, what level of performance do they display?

- market benchmarks – what are other people doing in similar functions in other similar companies?
- calculated benchmarks – based on our capacity planning exercise, it is possible to calculate a basic benchmark and then adjust it for a particular situation.

Example: Processing a specific transaction takes ten minutes; therefore, a person can handle six transactions per hour. To allow for natural breaks in the process we may then choose to establish a calculated benchmark at five transactions per hour and set this as an MPS.

Example: The average time for assembling a particular component may be forty minutes plus twenty minutes to test it and run quality control checks. Thus a calculated benchmark may be eight components per day with an MPS of six to allow for breaks, collecting materials and so on.

Once a minimum performance standard has been established for one aspect of a job you then repeat the process for the next aspect and so on, until each and every aspect of the job has been given an MPS.

There is a danger here: if you are under pressure on your goals (which is very probable in today's economic environment), there is a temptation to set the MPSs unrealistically high in an attempt to boost performance – this is *not* the function of the MPSs, it is the function of the goals. If the MPSs are set too high, then it is likely to result in unrealistic expectations about your people and an inability to assign the right people to the position. It is important, therefore, to test each MPS to ensure it is realistic.

Again, this is where the professionals in the Human Resources department can help as they are experienced in assessing such things. You could also go to someone who is already doing the job concerned to a satisfactory level and obtain their feedback – after all, a person experienced in the role will soon tell you whether the minimum performance standards are realistic.

The following are some examples of Minimum Performance Standards:

> 'To report all new business written during the month, on the Salesman Activity Report, by the third working day of the following month.'

(You will notice that this MPS states both the **responsibility** – the reporting of the new business written – and the **MPS** – on a particular form by a specific time.)

> 'To spend one day per month in face-to-face field coaching with each member of the team.'

(The responsibility is face-to-face field coaching, the MPS is one day per month with each member of the team. Obviously, if you have thirty team members this would be unrealistic and should be adjusted accordingly.)

> 'To obtain one piece of new business from every five interviews undertaken with prospects.'

(This reflects the general responsibility of a salesperson – to obtain new business – and defines an MPS closing ratio of one in five. Remember, this is not a restriction but a minimum performance – the goals may require a closing ratio of one in three, for example.)

I must stress that these are MPS – Minimum Performance Standards – and belong in the Job Specification. They describe the responsibilities associated with the position and define the minimum standard associated with the performance of those responsibilities.

Obviously, a Minimum Performance Standard must be measurable or observable – otherwise it would be impossible to determine whether a person is meeting their MPS. You must, therefore, determine *how* you are going to measure/observe the performance – you must set up controls – and then you must use these controls to provide feedback on performance.

At this point you should have an accurate Job Specification and the acceptable MPS for each part of it. The next step is to prepare a Job Profile.

The Job Profile

The Job Profile is a description of the principal behavioural characteristics that a person has to display to carry out the job to the minimum performance standards.

In trying to determine behavioural characteristics we are in the field of psychology – but help is at hand: there is a wide range of Human Resource tests available. But before they can be applied, we need to know what *we* are looking for: do we want someone who can work on their own and has self-discipline (characteristics necessary in a salesperson working away from the office, for example), or are we looking for someone with managerial attributes (because we need them to take responsibility for a project)?

The starting point, of course, is the Job Specification – what sort of person will be able to do that job to those specifications. A useful way of starting is to make an attempt to define the characteristics you would want to see in that person. To help you, there are a number of 'tools', and I have included the following questionnaire as one of the most useful:

Staff Characteristics Profile

On the following pages is a list of behavioural criteria. These criteria have been arrived at as a result of some twenty years of research into job performance criteria for many thousands of jobs of a wide variety of types. For convenience they have been arranged into five broad groupings, A to E.

Each criterion has been carefully defined to minimise overlap and to ensure there is a common understanding of what is meant by the criterion title. It is very important that you work with these definitions to prevent possible confusion.

Instructions

1 Consider carefully the job you wish to have filled. Review the Job Specification carefully with particular emphasis on the role of the job, its prime objectives and areas of key accountability, its organisational context, and its work priorities. Consider what you view as good or poor performance in the role and the basis for promotion in the job.

2 Consider the behavioural characteristics given and prioritise in terms of what you think are the most important behavioural characteristics for a person in that job. Do this for each grouping.

3 Finally, from your prioritised listing, select the twelve criteria you consider the most important for success in the job. You do not have to have equal numbers of criteria from each group and you do not have to prioritise your final selection.

Work through each grouping in order, A to E.

Group A – Individual behaviours

1. FLEXIBILITY. Ability to modify approach/style in order to reach a goal.

2. ADAPTABILITY. Ability to maintain effectiveness with changing environments, tasks, responsibilities, or people.

3 TENACITY. Ability to stay with a problem or line of thought until the matter is settled or the objective is no longer reasonably attainable—perseverance.

4. INDEPENDENCE. Actions based on own convictions rather than on a desire to please others. Willingness to question the party line.

5. COMPLIANCE. Adherence to company and/or procedures. Seeks approval from correct authority for changes.

6. INTEGRITY. Ability to maintain social, organisational, and ethical norms in job-related activities.

7. RISK TAKING. Extent to which calculated risks are taken. To gain recognised benefit or advantage deliberate gambles are necessary.

8. DECISIVENESS. Readiness to make decisions, render judgement, and take actions.

9. STRESS TOLERANCE. Stability of performance under pressure and/or opposition. Ability to make controlled responses in stressful situations.

Order of priority: 1 2 3 4 5 6 7 8 9
                   ... ...

Group B – Interpersonal behaviours

10. SOCIABILITY. Ability to mix easily with other people. Outgoing, participative.

11. IMPACT. Ability to create a good first impression on others and to maintain that impression.

12. ACCEPTABILITY. Personal style not likely to be abrasive to colleagues or customers.

13. INTERPERSONAL SENSITIVITY. Awareness of other people and environment and own impact on these. Actions indicate a consideration for the feelings and needs of others (but not to be confused with 'sympathy').

14. PERSUASIVENESS. Ability to make a persuasive, clear presentation of ideas or facts. Convince others to own expressed point of view, gain agreement or acceptance of plans, activities, or products.

15. TEAMWORK. Willingness to participate as a full member of

a team of which the job holder is not necessarily leader; effective contributor even when team is working on something of no direct personal interest.

16. WRITTEN COMMUNICATION. Ability to express ideas clearly in writing in good grammatical form.

17. ORAL COMMUNICATION. Effectiveness of expression in individual or group situations.

18. LISTENING. Ability to pick out important information in oral communications. Questioning and general reactions indicate to speaker 'active' listening.

Order of priority: 1 2 3 4 5 6 7 8 9
                   ... ...

Group C – Managerial behaviours

19. PLANNING AND ORGANISING. Ability to establish efficient and appropriate course of action for self and/or others to accomplish goal.

20. DELEGATION. Effective use of subordinates and other resources available. Knowledge of when, how, and whom to delegate. Effective allocation of decision-making and other responsibilities.

21. MANAGEMENT CONTROL. Appreciation of need for controls and maintenance of control over process, people, and tasks, and actions taken to ensure this.

22. LEADERSHIP. Ability to develop teamwork and maximise resources within a group to give most effective achievement of group objectives.

23. MANAGEMENT IDENTIFICATION. Ability to identify readily with and to accept the concerns and problems of management.

24. SUBORDINATE DEVELOPMENT. Developing the skills and

competencies of subordinates through training and development activities related to current and future jobs.

25. ORGANISATIONAL SENSITIVITY. Capacity to perceive the impact and implications of decisions and activities on other parts of the organisation.

26. ENVIRONMENTAL AWARENESS. Awareness of changing economic, social, and governmental environment likely to affect the job or the organisation. Well informed. Breadth and diversity of business-related knowledge.

Order of priority: 1   2   3   4   5   6   7   8
                       ... ...

Group D – Intellectual behaviours

27. PROBLEM ANALYSIS. Effectiveness in identifying problems, seeking pertinent data, recognising important information and identifying possible causes of problems.

28. CRITICAL THINKING. Ability to draw sound inferences from facts, recognise assumptions, discriminate between strong and weak arguments, reason logically by interpretation.

29. NUMERICAL ANALYSIS. Ability to analyse, organise and present numerical data, e.g. financial or statistical.

30. CREATIVITY. Ability to come up with imaginative solutions in business situations. Innovative. Capacity to identify radical alternatives to traditional methods and approaches.

31. JUDGEMENT. Ability to evaluate data and courses of action and to research logical decisions. Unbiased, rational approach.

32. PRACTICAL LEARNING. Assimilating and applying new, job-related information, taking into consideration rate and complexity.

33. DETAIL HANDLING. Tolerance for and ability to handle the details and paperwork associated with the job.

Order of priority: 1   2   3   4   5   6   7
                       ... ...

Group E – Motivational behaviours

34. SELF-MOTIVATION. The importance of work in attaining personal satisfaction. High need to succeed professionally.

35. CAREER AMBITION. Desire to advance to higher job levels; active efforts towards self-development for advancement. Career-minded.

36. COMMITMENT. Belief in own job or role, and its value to the organisation, makes the extra effort for the corporation though may not always be in own self-interest.

37. WORK STANDARDS. Setting of high goals or standards of performance for self, subordinates, others and organisation. Dissatisfied with average performance.

38. ENERGY. Ability to create and maintain a level of appropriately directed activity, capacity to work hard, drive, stamina.

39. INITIATIVE. Actively influencing events rather than passively accepting, sees opportunities and acts on them. Originates action.

40. RESILIENCE. Ability to maintain effectiveness in situations of disappointment and/or rejection.

Order of priority: 1   2   3   4   5   6   7
                       ... ...

Key Behaviour Characteristics

List what you feel are the twelve most important criteria for the job under review. Indicate both the criterion title and number. This listing does not have to be prioritized.

Number	Criterion title
....	....
....	....
....	....
....	....
....	....
....	....
....	....
....	....
....	....
....	....
....	....

Once you have done this, you need to check the validity of your choice. There are three very useful pieces of feedback you can obtain at this stage:

(i) you can compare your choice of characteristics with those displayed by someone already doing the job to your satisfaction

(ii) you can ask a colleague, whose opinion you respect, to review your choice and provide feedback, and

(iii) you can ask the Human Resource department for their opinion.

Having done this, you should review your choice, accepting or rejecting the suggestions arising from the feedback, and prepare your final Profile.

The Job Specification and the Job Profile together form the basis of recruitment – the process of obtaining the necessary human resource.

OBTAINING THE RESOURCE

Obtaining the resource can mean one of three things:

- recruiting a new member to the team to undertake the job
- re-assigning an existing team member to the job

or

- confirming an existing team member in a job.

Recruiting

Thousands of words have already been written on the subject of recruitment, interview techniques, selection procedures, and so on, and in most corporations this responsibility rests with the Human Resources department.

There are two sources on which you or your organisation can draw:

- internal (people already working within another department of the organisation who could be re-assigned into your team)
- external (people currently working for another organisation who could be attracted by advertising or by being 'head-hunted – i.e. they are known to you personally, are known to others helping you, or are found by an outside specialist firm).

Given the importance of commitment (discussed in Chapter 9), recruiting from within the organisation can often overcome the cultural problem – the person already knows about the organisation, probably sympathises with its aims, and knows 'the system'. On the other hand, bringing in someone from outside can inject a new dynamism as they are untainted by 'the system'.

In either case, I strongly recommend that you use the Human Resources department or an outside consultant to carry out all the initial identification of candidates and selection of those for interview. You should get involved only once a shortlist of suitable candidates has been selected. At this point, you should be reasonably certain that the candidates can do the job according to the specification and that they have the right profile.

Selection procedures generally involve:

- reviewing curriculum vitae or résumés
- inviting possible candidates for an initial interview
- selection and profiling tests
- a further review to select a shortlist
- a second in-depth interview in which you (as the person requiring the resource) participate along with the Human Resources interviewer
- a final selection
- an offer to the selected candidate (this may result in a further interview with you – concerning the detail of the job, to meet the team, and to visit the working environment; and a separate interview with Human Resources – to discuss the contractual details such as relocation, salary, pensions, holiday allowance and so on)
- an acceptance by the candidate.

You will notice that you should only be involved in the second selection interview and, after an offer has been made, in talking about the job itself and not about the contractual details.

Reassigning

To reassign an existing team member to a new job requires you to take the new Job Specification and Profile and then match each of your team against the profile. If you find someone with the right profile who is doing a different job then your first consideration must be to assess whether moving them will enhance the team's ability to achieve its objective – even though this may still leave you with a job position to fill.

Obviously, if moving a person will not enhance the team's ability to achieve its objective then reassignment is not an option.

Assuming that the reassignment is an option, you must consider whether the change in job assignment means a change in pay grade (again, Human Resources are the best guide) as this obviously has an impact on another resource – budget.

Even if the benefits of the reassignment outweigh the disadvantages, there are still other considerations that need to be weighed:

- Will the change in job benefit or disadvantage the person concerned in terms of their career? A move that is to someone's disadvantage has a demotivating effect that is seldom outweighed by an increase in pay.

- How will other team members react? The 'cost' of the investment of your time in handling adverse reactions may not be outweighed by the benefits to the organisation.

- Will the cost of retraining have an adverse impact on your budget that will not be outweighed by the benefits that accrue?

Having considered all these points, if you still decide to reassign then you will need to plan the training and support process until the person is settled. You will also have to plan the replacement of the person in their old job – if that job is considered necessary for the team to achieve its objectives.

Confirming an existing assignment

This is the most common result of the examination of your human resources. On the whole, if your objectives remain broadly the same as previously, then, providing your team generally achieves its goals, there is little incentive to change. However, this can be dangerous as a reassessment of people's development and a correct profiling may well show that greater benefits will accrue if people are reassigned.

Providing you have developed Job Specifications and Profiles for all necessary jobs within your team, and you have matched your people against the various profiles in an objective manner, you may well conclude that confirming people in their existing assignment is the best utilisation of the resources. After all, change just for the sake of change is not good management – it has to lead to additional benefits for both the person and the organisation.

ENSURING THE PERSON HAS THE RIGHT KNOWLEDGE

Having obtained and allocated your human resources, the next step is to ensure that they are equipped to carry out their responsibilities. An obvious statement, you may say, but one that is all too frequently overlooked – there is an assumption that, because we have selected them correctly, all members of our team can do what we ask of them. This is, quite simply, absurd. Our people have been selected on the basis that they have the right characteristics and, frequently, the right experience for the job but that does not mean they can do the job **in the way we want it done.** They have to be trained and, in some cases, retrained depending on the team's objectives.

Training falls into two categories:

- technical knowledge (how things work, how things are made, what things do, why processes exist, etc.)
- skills (how we do things).

Take selling widgets as an example: the salesperson needs to know all about the widget, what it can do, what its limitations are, what it is made of, how it is made, how much it costs, delivery time and a thousand and one other facts and figures all of which make up the salesperson's 'technical knowledge'. On the other hand, the salesperson must know how to sell, how to identify the customer's needs, how to discover sales opportunities, how to handle the customer's questions, how to negotiate, and how to close the sale – all of which make the 'skills' the salesperson needs to do the job.

I have frequently come across companies who provide the very minimum of basic training – normally in the technical knowledge area – and then expect the person to 'learn on the job'. This is false economy and generally leads to a dramatic failure to achieve goals. At the other end of the spectrum are those companies who spend so much time training their people that no one ever does any work earning money for the company.

The key is that everyone should have the skills and technical knowledge **to do the job to which they are assigned to the standard determined in the Job Specification.** This is the very minimum position. If you have tough goals to achieve, then your people may need to have more training, to have more technical knowledge and more skills. Either way, they need the knowledge and skills to achieve the objective which has been set.

Implementing Job Specifications

By this stage you will have new Job Specifications for all the positions within your team – and these may or may not match existing job descriptions. If there is a difference, and this is very likely if only because the new Job Specifications have MPSs attached, then each person will have to be provided with their new Job Specification and told how the changes affect them.

As all too many managers have discovered, changing a Job Specification can lead to all sorts of major complications with both team members and their unions (if they exist) – again, your Human Resources team can advise on this in terms of practicality and legality. Experience has shown that if fundamental changes are *imposed* in the work place, rebellion is the almost inevitable result, so care has to be taken in this area.

To come back to a point made at the beginning of this chapter, the construction of a Job Specification is a two-way process involving the manager (you) and the person doing the job. If you involve your people throughout the process of developing the specifications and minimum performance standards and show them how they are related to the team objectives and their own personal objectives, there is a good chance that the changes can be implemented without major problems.

Whatever the risks involved, the process of developing and implementing Job Specifications is one that must not be evaded because to avoid accepting the responsibility for the correct utilisation of your resources is to fail as a manger and a leader.

Annual Appraisals

Most members of large organisations regard the annual appraisal either with fear or with derision – the former because of unfair practices and the latter because it is perceived as meaningless. Both reactions show that the annual appraisal is not being conducted properly – generally, because of confusion as to what the annual appraisal is really for.

The primary function of the annual appraisal is to provide a structured forum during which the performance of the individual is reviewed objectively by comparison with the **responsibilities** and **minimum performance standards** defined in the Job Specification. As a result of this review, training requirements can be determined, potential promotions assessed, bonuses determined, and salary reviews agreed.

The annual appraisal is *not* the time to review performance against goals where these have been set to elicit a higher performance – this is the function of a 'performance review'. Unfortunately, most organisations try to run these two processes together, with the result that neither process is carried out satisfactorily.

Remember, a person who meets all the minimum performance standards for the job has earned the right to the job. However, he has not earned the right to a promotion, salary increase, bonus, if *all he has done* is meet the MPSs of the job – such benefits come the way of people who exceed the MPSs consistently. The really big financial rewards (annual bonuses, performance-related pay, and so on) are achieved by those who **not only exceed the MPSs of their job,** *but also* **exceed their performance-enchancing goals.**

Since you and the person concerned both know what the job responsibilities and the MPSs are, you will both know at any time whether they are being met. If they are not **then YOU should take action immediately** and not wait until the annual appraisal. Think of the consequences if an airline waited for an air crash before telling a pilot how to do the job properly.

If this constant monitoring of MPSs is carried out and corrective action taken immediately, the annual appraisal will contain no surprises either for the manager (you) or the team member. Instead, it becomes a time to discuss upgrading (with its associated higher MPSs), salary reviews, enhanced benefits, promotions or lateral changes to a different job, and so on. Reviewing training requirements (both technical and skills) can, and should, be carried out and action plans prepared to ensure the constant development of your team.

The annual appraisal is also a time for you to sit and listen to (and, if necessary, elicit) the team member's personal goals and career objectives as this will provide you with important data which can assist you when boosting motivation.

Forced ranking

No discussion of appraisals is complete without a brief look at the controversial subject of forced ranking. Developed during the 1970s and '80s, forced ranking was claimed to have a number of highly beneficial attributes. It was supposed to allow an organisation to weed out poor performances, to reward high flyers, and to ensure that the Human Resources budget was used most effectively. Unfortunately, all great ideas contain the seed of their own destruction, and forced ranking was no exception.

In its purest form, forced ranking required all staff to be graded on a scale of one ('badly under-performs') to five ('over-performs') in terms of their performance against the MPSs of the job. The theory was that this would allow all staff, irrespective of the job being done or the grade held, be compared and this would allow the identification of poor performers and the over-achievers. The theory was based on a normal statistical distribution curve (the traditional bell shape) whereby 10 per cent would be in grade one, 20 per cent in grade two, 40 per cent in grade three, 20 per cent in grade four, and 10 per cent in grade five. From this, according to the forced ranking proponents, an organisation would be able to get rid of the grade ones, train the grade twos, leave the grade threes, reward the grade fours, and promote and reward highly the grade fives.

The system, however, has three major faults:

- it relies on all staff populations having a statistical distribution of performers
- it assumes that under-performers (grade ones) should be got rid of, and that over-achievers (grade fives) should be rewarded
- it considers that people in different jobs with widely differing responsibilities can be compared as though like with like.

Let's take a closer look at these faults.

If managers are doing their job properly then under-performance, even partial under-performance, will be identified early and corrective action taken; thus, at the annual appraisal there should be no one falling into the grade one category and very few (nothing like 20 per cent of the 'population') in grade two. This would result in a distorted distribution curve with, perhaps, 5 per cent in grade two and 65 per cent in grade three – i.e. 65 per cent meet the MPSs attached to their job and 30 per cent exceed that standard. To achieve the objectives of forced ranking, however, managers are **forced** into **ranking** their staff inside a normal distribution curve resulting in a large proportion of staff being unfairly graded one and two and having their careers unfairly damaged. Since forced ranking is usually connected to remuneration bonuses, this results in a large proportion of staff being unfairly deprived of financial bonuses with a corresponding decline in motivation.

The assumption that grade ones should be got rid of and grade fives should be rewarded ignores the fact that a grade one performer could well be in the wrong job or has not been trained and that a grade five could have outgrown the job. In either case a good manager will have recognised this at a very early stage and will have adjusted the use of their human resources accordingly. Once again, at the annual appraisal it is unlikely there would be people who are performing well above or well below MPS.

Comparing the performance in different jobs is fraught with problems: how, for example, can you compare a top salesperson with performance-enhancing goals, who earns a corporation millions of dollars or pounds in profits, with a top secretary who has no profit-line impact and is unlikely to have anything other than MPSs to work against? Of course, it can be argued that both are vital to the organisation – and so they are – but is comparing them with each other fair and can it ever be communicated as being fair? Unfortunately, the normal result of such a comparison is demotivation on both sides.

All three faults cause forced ranking to fail in its objectives and they frequently result in a high degree of **demotivation**.

Finally, forced ranking totally ignores the impact of the manager on the performance of the team – a team led by a poor manager is likely to have fewer top performers than one led by a good manager – this results in the latter having more people earning bonuses than the former, which again results in demotivation among the team.

So, is forced ranking all bad and should it be scrapped?

Probably not is the answer, but it does need to be greatly modified. In an ideal world, the system would act as a check and balance for identifying good and bad management practices in the use of human resources. And, if connected to performance-related pay structures associated with *real* performance-enhancing goals, it would help identify *and grade* those who should be rewarded for their performance. But when it is used in the normal way it achieves very little and is usually counter-productive.

So what do we put in its place? The answer is **performance management, based on properly set goals, frequent performance reviews and feedback, and the correct support.** In this way, the very need for forced ranking is eliminated.

SUMMARY POINTS

- Your people are the most important resource available and, because they are amongst the most costly of resources, you must use them wisely.

- Every job must have a properly written, detailed Job Specification which defines the responsibilities of the job and contains specific Minimum Performance Standards against which performance will be monitored.

- Minimum Performance Standards (MPSs) are not the same as Goals, which are used to enhance performance.

- Each Job Specification should have a Job Profile which identifies the behavioural characteristics of the ideal person for the job.

- Using the Job Specification and the Job Profile, you must obtain the required resource by: (i) recruiting a new person, (ii) reassigning another team member to the role, or (iii) confirming in the role the person currently doing it.

- You must ensure that the human resource selected for the job has both the technical knowledge and the skills to do the job to the MPS – this is provided by training.

- The person's performance against the responsibilities and the MPS of the job must be monitored continuously and corrective action taken as soon as performance deteriorates from the MPS.

- Annual appraisals should contain no surprises either for the team member or for you, the manager.

- The annual appraisal is a structured forum during which performance of the individual is reviewed objectively so that training requirements can be identified, potential promotion assessed, bonuses determined, salary reviews agreed, and potential reassignments discussed.

- The main financial rewards resulting from the annual appraisal process should go to those who have *not only met their MPSs but have also exceeded their performance-enhancing goals.*

6

Team Development – Coaching and Training

Development phases • phase I – commitment and development • phase II – involvement and assimilation • phase III – maturity • phase IV – maintenance • developing your team • coaching for performance • training for development

JUST AS AN ATHLETE competes against steadily stronger opponents before trying for the Olympic title, you need to build up your performance and that of your team before 'going for gold'.

You can build performance in a number of ways – by developing key skills, taking on steadily more challenging goals, and building self-confidence – until improved performance becomes a natural and continuous part of your lives. However, experience in sports, in training pilots, and many other areas has shown that the development of performance goes in phases and at each phase appropriate performance management techniques need to be used.

DEVELOPMENT PHASES

Let's look at each phase in terms of the development of a sales team (although many of these points also apply to many other types of team in a business environment):

Development Phase I – Commitment and Development

A person in this phase of development is characterised by a lack of self-confidence in approaching customers, is fearful of rejection, may have a 'negative' attitude, does not have the appropriate face-to-face and telephone sales skills, lacks discipline in their approach to the market and their work, and relies heavily on colleagues and management for guidance, direction, support, praise, and help. People in this phase tend to have a strong aversion to being given individual goals.

On the positive side, the person is likely to be enthusiastic (but may not show it), is normally willing to learn, has a strong desire for training, is a willing team player, identifies with the team and their goals, takes guidance well and responds to positive feedback.

If we have people in this phase the key skills we have to use in managing them include positive feedback, training, clear communication of performance standards, clear definition of the individual's contribution to the team goals, group monitoring, group and one-to-one coaching sessions, and plenty of motivational talks.

Goals set at this stage are very short-term (possibly set on a daily or weekly basis) and will cover activity more than business acquisition. All goals must be sufficiently difficult to require steadily improved performance but easy enough to ensure that **no one fails to meet their goal** (achieving their goal gives confidence to take on a greater challenge).

Development Phase II – Involvement and Assimilation

People in phase II are characterised by a disciplined but 'plodding' approach to the market, they tend to be 'rule bound' and do everything 'by the book', they show little entrepreneurial inclination, administration seems to take up their time, they deal with customers professionally but without enthusiasm, they tend to be reactive (waiting for customers) rather than proactive (going and getting customers), customers seem to be considered an interruption to their work rather than the reason for it, individual activity goals are accepted but they prefer team business acquisition goals.

In this phase people are sensitive to criticism, only grudgingly accept corrective feedback, regard training as an evil necessity, are very suspicious of praise or positive feedback, and feel that any interest in them by the manager has to be negative.

The overall belief is that sales is a 'damned hard job and I don't know why I ever agreed to do it': however, suggest they change to something less stressful and the idea will be rejected. This is not a pleasant time either for the salesperson or for the manager – fortunately it tends to be reasonably short.

The key management skills needed here are good humour, a very balanced approach, consistent management support, firm but fair guidance and direction, openness (do not close up when 'attacked'), good one-to-one coaching, good corrective feedback (but neither to excess), a positive mental attitude, a motivational approach.

This phase builds on the foundations in phase I but the salesperson finds it difficult to believe they will ever see the final result.

Goals in this phase should include individual business acquisition goals along with sales activity goals. Weekly goals and monthly goals are the norm with regular (but unpressured) performance reviews. Goals should always be achieved but they should be steadily more challenging.

Development Phase III – Maturity

What characterises this phase the most, and sets the tone for the rest of the time, is the almost instantaneous transformation of the salesperson from a plodder to an enthusiastic, committed, highly motivated achiever. Suddenly, it seems that nothing is impossible, business comes in easily and stays on the books, relationships between the salesperson and customers are professional, respectful, and friendly. The salesperson now makes a positive contribution to the motivation of the team and openly and unselfishly helps others to achieve their goals. No longer is there a tendency to want all the business available to meet personal goals; the salesperson now knows there is plenty more and can afford to give business to others.

In this phase the salesperson sees training as desirable, a way of improving performance. Coaching and corrective feedback are welcomed, self-confidence is high, positive feedback is accepted as being due, and such feedback will probably be conveyed to colleagues to help them reach their goal.

Salespeople in this phase become highly goal-orientated, focusing on business acquisition goals, activity goals, and the team goals with equal intensity.

The key skills you need in dealing with people in this phase include coaching and corrective feedback, positive feedback, performance-challenging goal-setting, motivational support, professional friendship, and a willingness to recognise that one of your team may be better than you are.

Goals in this phase tend towards product-specific business acquisition goals (both monthly and quarterly), monthly sales activity goals with monthly performance reviews, and activity planning sessions. The goals should be very challenging and, although realistic and achievable, they may not always be met – this should not be criticised but used to motivate and challenge the individual.

Development Phase IV – Maintenance

It is an accepted fact that many salespeople never really want to be anything other than salespeople – they remain mature, positive, and highly motivated goal-achieving individuals but they remain in the job with little desire to go beyond. We have to recognise that such people are the backbone of a good sales team.

In this phase you continue to use the same skills as in Phase III and in much the same way – however, you have to watch out for demotivation and 'staleness' which come from repetition. You need to set even more challenging goals and you have to recognise good performance in a greater variety of ways.

Unfortunately, when salespeople reach this stage they tend to find that the challenge has gone out of the job – they feel they have achieved all there is to achieve in the role and, not being willing to change jobs, they seek other challenges. This results in our losing good salespeople.

If we are lucky, and our salespeople are willing to go on to other challenges within sales management, it is in this phase that they will start to display the necessary leadership and management potential and we must capitalise on this immediately. We should look to place such people in charge of small teams (product-specific or market-specific are two possibilities) and encourage them to develop their management skills through training and by coaching them on a regular basis.

For salespeople leading sales teams we have to be careful with goal-setting – the individual will take their own goals but these may be smaller than before, and they will also take responsibility for the team goals.

Clearly, each member of a team develops at a different rate and at any point there will be individuals in each of the development phases. Generally speaking, the distribution is likely to be in the region of: 20 per cent phase I; 40 per cent phase II; 30 per cent phase III, and 10 per cent phase IV. You, as the manager, have to ensure that each member of your team develops steadily through the phases and that you always have new people coming forward. If you lose a top performer from phase III or IV you should aim to push a phase II/III person to replace them and bring new people in at the bottom – in this way you do not import 'prima donnas' who may be disruptive and you give your team a clearly defined career structure.

Having the majority of our team in phases I and II means, however, that the pressure is on us to develop and use the skills and personal attributes that will see us through as successful 'people developers' – as successful and effective Performance Managers.

Developing your team

There are two key activities you will need to use in the development of your team – coaching and training. Both provide structured assistance to team members either individually or as part of a small group but they fulfil different functions. In both cases, the subjects to be improved are identified during regular performance reviews and during the annual appraisal.

Coaching, as an activity, is different from training. Coaching is a one-to-one or small-group activity focusing on specific skills or on product knowledge and is carried out either 'on the job' or off-line but within the normal working environment. Coaching is one of your responsibilities as team leader and you should deliver it to your team.

Training, on the other hand, is the formal process of imparting knowledge and skills; it is almost always carried out in small groups (eight to twenty people) away from the normal work environment. Because of the nature of the training process, training is generally delivered by professional trainers who specialise in the delivery of particular training programmes – they may be drawn from line management but the programme leader is almost always a specialist trainer.

Coaching for performance

There are, essentially, two types of coaching: the first is generally skill- or product-specific and is delivered following (or as a result of) the team member making a mistake which you have spotted. The second is more general and forms part of an overall, longer-term development programme and is sometimes called 'field training'. Both types of coaching are based on an assumption that you know what your team members are supposed to be doing and how they are supposed to be doing it – as the team leader you should have a good knowledge of everything that your team is supposed to do; without this knowledge you will lack the credibility to coach and may even lack the credibility to be effective as the team leader.

Coaching a specific subject

Although you will be correcting errors when you see them, occasionally this will be insufficient, especially where the problem concerns lack of knowledge or skill. When this occurs you should attempt to coach the particular skill or product knowledge. The following structure will help you carry this out but is not meant to be restrictive. As you become practised in its use, you will find that the whole coaching discussion takes very little time and that the first three steps may take only a few minutes.

Step 1 – Position the discussion. Arrange for the individual to have a one-to-one private meeting with you – remember to tell them that the meeting is to develop and implement a coaching session on a specific subject. When the individual arrives you should restate the purpose of the meeting and then describe the current performance versus the desired or expected performance – this should be done in terms of the specific skill or product knowledge area that has attracted your attention.

Step 2 – Investigate the situation. Having described what you have observed, compared with what you consider to be a desirable performance, you should encourage the individual to talk about it. Using probing skills such as open-ended questions, get the team member to tell you what they consider to be the problem. Spend time clarifying your understanding and ensuring that the two of you are in agreement over the situation. Discuss the desired performance in terms of the benefits to the individual.

You should then confirm that there is a need to correct the performance and you should obtain their agreement to that need. This is a very important point since the coaching will only be successful if the person sees a need to change.

Step 3 – Explore solutions. Encourage the individual to tell you what they think should be done in terms of coaching and offer alternative solutions that may be more appropriate. Select the best solution and confirm agreement.

Step 4 – Action. If the best solution to the developmental need is for further training or if the need itself is more complex, then the two of you should develop an action plan and put it into operation. However, if the individual is a reasonably experienced member of the team then most developmental needs can be dealt with without resorting to training programmes.

Assuming that the solution chosen is to coach the skill or product knowledge, you have two choices: either spend time there and then to coach, or set up a separate meeting if time is a bit short. My preferred approach is to coach immediately while the individual's mind is focused on the need for improvement.

(i) Put the skill (or knowledge) being coached into perspective. Identify where in the process the skill belongs.

(ii) Explain the skill and how it works in relation to the rest of the process. If it is a multi-part skill then explain each part.

(iii) Give practical examples of the skill and role-play it to demonstrate its use.

(iv) Get the individual to role-play the skill until they are 'word perfect'.

(v) Allow the individual to role-play the whole process with the new skill in place.

(vi) Repeat the last two steps until you are satisfied they have acquired the skill.

Step 5 – Conclusion and follow-up. Express your confidence in the individual's ability to use the skill correctly and establish the follow-up process:

- you will observe the individual for a while to ensure the skill is being used correctly, and
- the coaching will be repeated as often as necessary to ensure the skill is thoroughly learned.

This follow-up process is very important as it enforces two things vital to the success of any coaching:

(i) it tells the individual that improved performance is the norm and that the correct use of skills is part of the Minimum Performance Standard for the job, and

(ii) it ensures that any reversion to unacceptable performance is picked up very quickly and re-coached. This reinforces the message that you, as the manager, are continuously monitoring performance and that development work is not a one-off event.

Coaching as a general development programme

Irrespective of having identified specific development needs, you should always spend a specific period of time with each member of your team as part of a general development process. Sometimes called 'field training', this type of coaching programme involves you in spending a 'typical' day with a member of your team to the exclusion of everything else. Such time should be scheduled in advance and should occur on a regular basis – perhaps once a month with someone new to a position, perhaps once a quarter with someone who is experienced in the role – and everyone should be involved.

If no coaching programme is in existence, then I suggest you introduce the concept during one of your regular team meetings, taking care to explain what is involved, how it works, and the benefits to them (i.e. a chance to receive advice and help, to receive on-the-spot coaching, to introduce you to their work so that a full understanding is obtained). You should ensure that they understand that they will always be 'in charge' of the process, sales interview, meeting, or whatever is involved: you will only observe the process at the time and will not participate actively at all.

This last point must be stressed to ensure that a coaching day is not confused with a day in which you, as the manager, are involved with the process. For example: a sales interview, in which it is necessary for you to participate to ensure the sale, is not suitable as a coaching occasion.

Once the coaching programme has been introduced and the criteria have been established, the process is as follows:

Step 1 – Preparation. Arrange with the team member which day you will spend with them – this should be a date about a week in advance.

The team member must arrange suitable interviews, or other 'normal' activities.

A few days before the coaching day, you should review the proposed programme with the team member to ensure:

(i) they have prepared properly, with an adequate number of activities or meetings and sufficient time to provide feedback after each one, and

(ii) you understand what is going to happen during the day.

Step 2 – Briefing. Before the day gets under way, you should review the team member's preparation for any activity involving clients, either directly in a meeting or indirectly (i.e. work to be done on a client's behalf). You should check:

- the client information
- the aim of the meeting or activity

- the anticipated needs of the client or the opportunities that are being looked for
- the expected client attitude towards the meeting and any proposal that is to be put forward.

It is wise to review the roles you will both play – the team member is in charge, you will be an observer. You should also agree how you will be introduced to the client to ensure acceptance of your presence.

Step 3 – Observation. Allow the team member to introduce you and to explain why you are there. Mention to the client (or others involved in the meeting) that you will be taking notes in your role as an observer.

Keep unobtrusively in the background and out of eye contact with either the client or the team member – take notes of key points only.

If you are spoken to by either the team member or the client during the meeting always turn it back to the team member – do not offer assistance or advice except to confirm facts. (Warning: many managers feel compelled to intervene if a client interview is going wrong and they give 'saving the sale' as a reason; unfortunately, this destroys the purpose of the coaching process as they cease to be an observer. While no hard-and-fast rule can apply, the temptation to intervene should be resisted strongly as a 'failure', or temporary setback, is likely to prove an invaluable learning opportunity.)

At the end of the meeting make a point of thanking the client personally for allowing you to sit in.

Step 4 – Debriefing. Immediately following the meeting, if possible, you and your team member should debrief the call while it is still fresh in your minds.

In debriefing a coaching call, you do *not* give your opinion about what was done well or badly; rather, you ask your team member to give their analysis of:

- what skills were handled well

- what skills could have been handled more effectively.

Once you have obtained their analysis, you then provide feedback from your observation. If there is time you could even reconstruct the whole meeting. Either way, your feedback should:

- summarise which skills you feel were handled well, and
- summarise which skills need improvement.

If both of you agree on what needs improvement it may be possible to coach the skill immediately, time permitting, using the approach outlined above. If this is not possible, then you should agree a date and time when the coaching will take place.

Training for development

Training is the formal teaching of skills or product knowledge – but it is also rather more than that. Training is the backbone of all performance because it is through training that our team learn the basic skills they need to do their job and meet the Minimum Performance Standards (MPSs) that have been set.

In some companies, training is a one-off process that takes place when a person first joins the organisation or takes on a new function. For these organisations training tends to be seen as a costly necessity and most 'training' is done 'on the job'. Further formal training is only offered if a person is moved from one technical job to another technical job.

Even in more enlightened organisations, skills training tends to be restricted to the basic skills with little attempt to impart more advanced skills. This places an undue burden on the team members, who often have to struggle to acquire advanced skills on their own, and on the managers who are forced into delivering a process (training) that they are ill-equipped to provide.

Managers are responsible for coaching the skills already taught in formal training to ensure that they are being delivered to the MPS for that job – it is unrealistic to assume that managers can automatically deliver a high level of training in skills, and organisations that fail to realise this display little understanding of the differing roles of training and coaching in the development of their people.

Some companies and organisations (such as airlines) require all their staff to undergo refresher training or advanced training on a regular basis and frequently link grade promotions and functional promotions to the successful completion of specific courses. These organisations tend to have a centralised training department staffed by training professionals.

If your company views training as a one-off process, or is too small to have its own training department, it is your responsibility to ensure that a way is found to overcome the shortcoming. This can be done by the use of outside training consultants, of which there is now a very wide variety covering just about every possible area of training that you may require. Specialist consultants are, however, quite expensive in budget terms and you will need to be careful in your allocation of budgeted resources if you are going to make use of them. Another alternative is to put together your own training programme using training material such as films, videos, audio tapes and books, all of which are generally available either from specialist suppliers or from consultancies.

Whichever route you have to take, you must plan your team's training programme to make maximum use of budget and to minimise the adverse impact of keeping people away from their jobs. However, you also need to consider the trade-off of improved performance that results almost immediately from good training against the short-term problems of having team members away. A properly planned and implemented training programme is a motivational tool provided the individuals concerned can see the benefit to them (i.e. improved performance, promotion, a higher grade, improved prospects).

Training is a direct investment in your people and like all investment it must have a defined objective and a clear, measurable or observable return. In today's environment of tight budget controls, sending your people on training programmes in exotic locations as a form of reward does not make good business sense unless the training has a direct practical relevance to that person's job and the performance of the team in general.

Finally, do not forget to plan your own training programme at the same time as that of your team. All too few companies invest in training their managers – there is an assumption that once you become a manager you know all there is to know about your job – but managers need to improve their skills all the time in what is a highly competitive environment. And the same points apply to you as to your team – your training must be relevant and must provide a return on the investment.

SUMMARY POINTS

- The development of performance goes in phases and at any one time your team members will be in different phases.
- Each development phase requires a different performance management approach and different management skills.
- There are two principal development activities: training and coaching.
- Training is the formal teaching of essential skills.
- Coaching is the maintenance of skills through one-to-one coaching activity and through coaching programmes.
- You are responsible for ensuring your people are trained – but training is best done by professionals and arranging it

should be the responsibility of the training department.

- Coaching is your direct responsibility as the manager – it cannot be delivered by anyone else.

7

Motivation

Motivation or manipulation ● *incentives* ● *the ten laws of motivation*

MOTIVATION OR MANIPULATION?

OVER THE YEARS a great deal has been written and spoken about motivation. Companies talk about needing highly motivated staff, needing managers who are self-motivated self-starters, and needing to be motivational places in which to work. But ask them to define motivation and you will receive a wide range of answers.

Rather than wade through the hundreds of definitions, I think it would be easier to explain what I mean by motivation since this definition is the basis of performance management. I define **motivation** as

> 'getting someone to do what THEY want'

and I define **manipulation** as

> 'getting people to do what WE want'.

Since people only do things that benefit themselves (either psychologically or materially) they will be happy to be motivated but will have little interest in being manipulated – and in extreme cases, they will actively reject it.

Unfortunately, many managers do not understand the destructive long-term effect of manipulation and see only the short-term benefits that accrue, so let us take a brief look at manipulation and why it does not work in the long term.

Manipulation – getting people to do what **we** want – is generally coercive; it is based on **making people do things they may not normally want to do** so that *we* achieve *our* goals. In the process of manipulating people we ignore what *they* want to do, thus indicating to them that their goals are of little or no importance to us and, somewhat naturally, they do not like this. And if their goals are not important to us, why should our goals be important to them? Now, it is important to understand that manipulation is *not* the same as giving orders or adopting a directive management style where this is appropriate – such a style is accepted providing that the ultimate goal of the manager and his team members are the same.

'But,' I hear some people say, 'surely the goal of the manager and the goal of his team members are always the same?' Not so. If we look beyond the ostensible team goal (to bring in a certain volume of sales, to process orders within a certain time, to build machines to do a specific job, to make a better widget, and so on) **the manager's personal goal** is likely to be the status and rewards that come from achieving the team goal – we may achieve a pay rise, a promotion, a bigger office, our own parking space, more responsibility; on the other hand, **the team member's personal goal** may be to get paid so that they can take a better holiday, buy their family the things they want, and have an adequate income to enjoy life. If the truth be known, **they** are *likely* to achieve their personal goals **even if the team fails to achieve its goal**, whereas **we** are *not likely* to achieve our personal goals **unless the team reaches its goal**.

In these circumstances, if you try to *make* the team members reach the team goal (so that you achieve your goals) you will be manipulating them and they are unlikely to respond in a positive manner, so you fail in your objective.

Equally, if you threaten their ability to achieve their personal goals by threatening to fire them, reduce their pay, or downgrade them unless they achieve the team goal, you are again trying to manipulate them and they will react negatively in the longer term, although they may well react 'positively' in the short term. Threats, as a method of achieving increased performance, can be used once and might as well not be used at all given the negative reaction and negative feelings that are generated.

If the primary management philosophy in a company is based on manipulation, the long-term effect is likely to be declining performance, increased absenteeism, a high level of industrial unrest and strikes, employee sabotage, an inability to attract new staff or staff of the right calibre, a high level of staff attrition, declining staff attitudes towards the customers, and eventually an inability to compete in the marketplace. Such a cycle of decline has been obvious in a number of advanced industrial countries and is all too apparent in the underdeveloped economies of Eastern Europe.

Manipulation as a management philosophy belongs (if it should ever have been allowed to exist) to the first half of the century. It is sad to see it still in existence in some companies in the 1990s, but we are unlikely to see the philosophy, or those companies that use it, surviving into the 21st century. Motivation, on the other hand, is a powerful driving force – in fact, it is behind everything we do: without it not a wheel turns, not a dollar is made, nothing is done. So what is this tool?

Motivation – getting people to do what **they** want – is the reason they do anything, the reason for all their actions, and at the very basic, lowest level it has to do with survival. Once we have addressed our need for survival – having enough food for ourselves and our family, a home to live in, clothes to wear – the next level is to achieve what we consider to be a reasonable standard of living – a car, a television, a stereo system, holidays, leisure activities; then we look at achieving social status at a personal level, and finally we look at our professional activities.

(Maslow, in his study of motivation, took this one stage further and developed his theory of the Hierarchy of Needs which has five levels. These start with Basic Physiological Needs (survival), after which we address Safety and Security Needs, Social and 'Belongingness' Needs, Esteem Needs, and finally, Self-Actualisation Needs.)

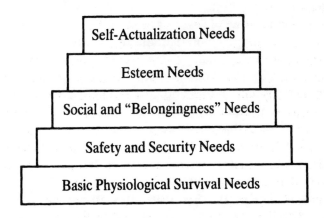

Maslow's Hierarchy of Needs

Clearly, if we are motivated to survive, then survival becomes our personal goal. And all the other things we are motivated to achieve also become personal goals: however, you will notice that there are many personal goals that precede achieving a professional or work-related goal. The fact that we have these personal goals helps us establish one of the Laws of Motivation – **motivation requires a goal**. Unless someone has a clearly defined goal, they will not be motivated.

Now, many managers will tell you that what really motivates people is money – but this is a fallacy: except for King Midas, no one is motivated purely by money – but they are motivated by the things money will allow them to do. If you look again at the points above it becomes clear that most of the personal goals (survival, standard of living, etc.) can be achieved by having enough money, but once those goals are met money has little further value as an aid to motivation. For many people, once they have ensured survival and achieved their desired standard of living, there is little else they want and they become happy to stroll through life without worrying about having more money – for these people money no longer aids motivation.

'But', I hear some of yesterday's managers say, 'if that is the case, why do people go on demanding pay rises?' The answer is straightforward: if their company is offering nothing else in terms of motivation, and they have no other clearly defined goals at the social status and professional level, then more money becomes the only thing they can strive for. Research strongly suggests that once people are satisfied with their level of pay, can meet their survival needs and desired standard of living, they become less motivated by money and place a higher emphasis on higher-order rewards. In these circumstances, money becomes a form of **recognition**. This gives us a second Law of Motivation – **motivation requires recognition.**

Incentives

At this point, I think we should take a quick look at incentives – those schemes in which managers place so much faith and yet so often fail in their objective: to motivate the team. Incentives and incentive schemes are great favourites, particularly in sales environments, because they address one of the laws of motivation – 'motivation needs recognition'. However, for incentives to work they need to follow some basic rules:

Everyone must be able to 'win' the incentive. To make this possible, the trigger point for the incentive must either be reachable by all levels of performer – in which case it is likely to be so low that it is valueless – or the incentive must be triggered by reaching a certain percentage of a goal.

Incentives must be very publicly awarded. The incentive has no value if the only people who know about it are the winner sand their manager.

The best incentives have high status value but low monetary value. One of the best incentive schemes, and one of the most powerful and successful, was the 'Salesman of the Month Award' in IBM – the winner received a certificate and a $2 model of a *rubber duck* to display on their desk! Another successful scheme awarded the winner lunch with the chief executive officer of the business during which the CEO invited the winner to talk about their work.

Cash bonuses are NOT motivational and are poor incentives. If people are awarded cash bonuses they tend to come to rely on the money and have pre-spent it and view it as part of the pay package – plus the fact that, in most countries, cash bonuses are taxed at the highest rate of tax for that individual.

Commission incentive schemes do work. Commission incentive schemes work well for those involved: however, those not involved can often become demotivated. The schemes can also be expensive and difficult to administer and can degenerate into chaos which becomes demotivational.

Incentive schemes should be short-term and linked to the sales cycle. Like goals, incentive schemes work best if limited to a maximum of three months before the award. This is ideal when linked to a sales cycle (product launch, a seasonal downturn).

But what about Maslow's other 'needs' – Safety and Security, Status and Belongingness, and Self-Actualisation? These, along with the need for Esteem, are not easily satisfied by money and in most cases cannot be satisfied by money at all. Safety and Security are normally met by job security and fringe benefits; Status and Belongingness can come from a position in the local community as well as from membership of a team within a business; the need for Esteem is another way of saying 'the need for recognition'; and Self-

Actualisation is supplied by challenging tasks calling for creativity.

For your team to be fully motivated, they need to have met each level of personal goal, each level in the hierarchy of needs. Obviously, each person will be focusing on a different level of need at any one time and will be motivated by different things. They may even refocus on a lower-level need if they feel it is at risk (for example, if a survival need is threatened by a manipulative manager). Research suggests that until each level of need is satisfied, people will not focus on a higher level. However, there is little evidence to suggest that all needs within a level must be satisfied before people will move to the next level.

As a performance manager, you should always be aware of the fact that what motivates an individual will change over time and that each individual in your team is motivated by different, although frequently similar, things.

However, enough of the theory. Let us look at the Ten Laws of Motivation so that you can develop a clear picture of what you must do to motivate your team.

THE TEN LAWS OF MOTIVATION

1. WE need to be motivated to motivate others

Unless you are charged up and enthusiastic there is no way you will be able to motivate others. Your attitude and your mood directly affects the attitude and mood of those you work with. If you are feeling low, out of sorts, or demotivated, your people will catch the atmosphere and become demotivated themselves – if you are full of enthusiasm then your people are more likely to be enthusiastic.

To illustrate this I want you to imagine walking into a large room. At one end is a group of your colleagues who are talking enthusiastically, perhaps laughing, and generally having a good time. At the other end of the room is a similar sized group who are talking very quietly together, with little enthusiasm. Which group is the one you are more likely to move towards? If you are anything like the majority of people, you will head rapidly towards the first group and avoid the second.

This illustration also applies to individuals: most of us, at some time or another, have had to work with managers or colleagues who are moody, unmotivated sorts of people. After a while, we begin to avoid their company and seek excuses for not having to deal with them. And when we do have to talk to them, we come away feeling turned off, shut down, and demotivated.

If you are to avoid adversely affecting your staff you need to control your feelings, hide the negative, promote a positive mental attitude, and project your enthusiasm for the work in hand. You must be seen to be supporting the team goals (and, by extension, the corporate goals) and to be working towards them even when there are very good reasons why you may be feeling low – for example, personal problems, illness, a family crisis. In these circumstances, to avoid spreading your temporary lack of motivation to your team, my advice is to set to work on some project that does not involve working with others. Once your people see you working solidly at something they are less likely to interrupt you with anything except the most serious problems. In this way your team will probably assume that your withdrawn attitude is to do with the work you are focused on rather than a lack of personal motivation.

2. Motivation requires a goal
Unless a person really knows where he is going he will not know in which direction to go. People need to know what they are trying to achieve and to really want to achieve it – then they will be motivated. We will be looking at the whole subject of goals in greater detail in chapter 9.

3. Motivation is in two stages:

(i) Find a person's goal in relation to the team goal.

(ii) Show them how to get it.

The key here is the person's goal *in relation to the team goal* – your objective as a performance manager is to motivate your people so that the team goals are achieved (after all, that is what you are being paid for – it is your direct responsibility).

But you must avoid manipulation. To do this you must persuade them that what they want to achieve is part of what the team wants to achieve and you must do it without trying to make them do something they would not normally want to do – in many ways, you must sell them on the idea of the team goals and show them how what they want will contribute.

4. Motivation, once established, never lasts

This is an unfortunate truth and one of which many managers are unaware. They think that all they have to do is motivate their people at the start of the process and that will carry them through. Generally speaking, the level of motivation declines over time and, for most, businesses motivation will sink gradually to zero over a period of three to six months.

You need to recognise this and become a professional motivator, constantly feeding motivation into your team through regular team meetings, clear communications, recognition, and frequent one-to-one feedback sessions. In many ways, this is the key to successful performance management.

5. Motivation requires recognition

We have already touched on this when discussing Maslow's Hierarchy of Needs – once basic needs are met, the need for recognition increases. In fact, psychologists have found that people work harder for recognition than they do for money. All your people need to have the opportunity to earn recognition, they crave it, and once it has been earned it must be clearly, publicly, and promptly given.

But you can only recognise a **result** and must not try to give recognition for an **effort**. You must avoid congratulating people for being 'a good worker' or for 'making the greatest [generally undefined] contribution to the business' – such recognition is devalued in the eyes of the receiver and the eyes of the rest of the team.

6. Participation motivates
Participating in a special project or specific team is highly motivational. If the team has a cause and the team members are committed to it then they will be motivated. You use this rule when you obtain the individual's commitment to the team goals.

7. Seeing your own progress is motivational
Individuals are highly motivated by being able to see their own progress towards their goals – we all like to see how we are doing, but it is important that we see our progress against our own goals and not those of others. However, if we see our progress in terms of a percentage of our individual goal then it is also motivational to see how others are progressing towards their goals. Seeing our progress allows us to *experience* our success – and our future success is built on an experience of success.

8. Competition only motivates if we can win
Competitions are frequently used as incentives but they only work when everyone has an equal chance of winning. If there is not an equal chance of winning, the top people will be motivated and the rest will be highly demotivated. This problem can be avoided by measuring competitive performance in terms of percentage of individual goal. When running competitions many organisations set the target as an absolute goal, for example, a sales competition winner may be the person who sells the greatest number of products in a set period of time. This is likely to be demotivational to people new to the sales team because they perceive that the top performers

are always likely to win in these circumstances and that there is no point in them competing. On the other hand, if the winner was the person who had achieved the greatest percentage above their own sales goal, this would allow anyone to win because the newcomer would have a lower goal than a top performer and both would have to produce an outstanding performance to pass their goal and win the competition.

9. There is a motivational spark in everyone

Contrary to popular belief (and observation), there is a motivational spark in everyone. Everyone can be motivated, some more easily than others, but that spark is there – as a performance manager you have to find that spark, nurture it, and fan it into a flame. Since motivation of your team is a prime managerial responsibility, finding the motivational spark in every member of the team becomes an activity of great importance if you are to succeed.

10. 'Group-belonging' motivates

People are motivated by working as part of a team towards a team goal – but only if they have 'bought in' to that goal.

SUMMARY POINTS

- Motivation is getting people to do what THEY want to do.
- Manipulation is trying to get people to do what YOU want them to do.
- Your primary responsibility is to persuade your team members to want what you want.
- Everyone is motivated to achieve their personal goals; they must satisfy their basic needs before they will be motivated to achieve business goals.

- People work harder for recognition than they do just for money.
- There are ten simple Laws of Motivation:
    1 You need to be motivated to motivate others.
    2 Motivation requires a goal.
    3 Motivation is in two stages, identifying personal goals and showing how they can be attained.
    4 Motivation, once established, never lasts.
    5 Motivation requires recognition.
    6 Participation motivates.
    7 Seeing your own progress is motivational.
    8 Competition only motivates if you can win.
    9 There is a motivational spark in everyone.
    10 'Group-belonging' motivates.

Part III
Achieving the objective

The planning has been done, the resources allocated, the team assembled, the training complete – now is the time to achieve the objective, which is the whole point of our work. You may consider it pedantic to state that achieving the objective is the whole point of our work but look around you at people going about their daily working lives – the way they move, the way they act, the way they manage often makes me wonder what is their objective and whether achieving it is important at all. While there is no doubt that each manager has been given a target to achieve during the year, it is clear that few of them are motivated to achieve it and most are probably just 'serving their time'.

This unfortunate state of affairs arises, I believe, as a result of failure in three key areas vital to performance management and to the well-being of your team and your company: **communication, objective setting,** and **performance feedback**. If you are to achieve success as a performance manager then competence in these three areas must be a primary goal.

8
Office environment – Physical and Psychological

The physical environment • the psychological environment – communication • what has to be communicated, and to whom • the way information is communicated

THE PHYSICAL ENVIRONMENT

IN CHAPTER 1 we took a brief look at the impact a person's physical environment has on their ability to produce an optimum performance and we noted that offices that are too hot, too cold, or insufficiently well lit have a negative impact on people's work. We also saw that the non-work environment of the office (the toilets, the kitchen area, etc.) also impact on how we think about the company as a place to work. A poor working environment translates into opinion in the form of *'If they don't care about the conditions in which we have to work, how can they really care about us?'*

This subject is well recognised by most organisations and a great deal of time, effort, and money is spent on developing a pleasant working environment. Some companies even go to the extent of relocating to a rural area to encourage their staff to feel that going to work is a pleasant experience. Governments have also got in on the act – in a reaction to the 'dark satanic mills' of the industrial revolution and Dickensian England, legislation has been passed to establish the minimum and maximum temperatures permitted in an office, to define how much space each person must have, what light must be available, and what level of noise is acceptable in any situation. In some continental European countries the laws relating to working environments are so complex that just about everything about an office, factory, shop, or warehouse is controlled.

Although we might question the need for such restrictive laws, the basic philosophy is understandable and few business leaders rebel. However, some companies take the whole subject to almost lunatic extremes and have rules defining what type of chairs, desks, lights, pictures, etc., each person can have. One well-known bank used to have rules that made it clear that junior managers could not have a carpet, nor could they have a chair with arms – for all I know, these rules may still apply. Stories abound of companies that require secretaries to occupy large, open-plan and extremely noisy offices while the managers each have individual offices.

Things are changing, however, and one major computer company has recently opened their new headquarters in a building that has no assigned spaces and no individual offices – each person checks in each morning, collects their 'office' (a wheeled trolley containing all their files) and locates where they want to work that day. On arrival at their 'station' they log into the computer on the desk and this automatically causes their electronic mail and telephone calls to be routed to the correct location. Such flexible working environments may not suit all companies but it is an interesting concept worth exploring.

As a team leader you have to do the best you can for your team within the space and rules applicable to your company. But if you want your people to perform well, you need to ensure that they have the necessary tools and equipment and a suitable environment in which to work. Generally speaking, in an office-based environment this means you will need to assess exactly what they will need in the way of desks, chairs, filing systems, telephones, calculators, computers, etc. to do their job at the level that will allow the team to meet their goals. Obviously, if the team is dispersed during the working day – for example, a sales team or technology and computer support people – then they will have different needs and these should be examined carefully to ensure that the lack of tools does not hold them back.

If you have the opportunity, and your company's policy is flexible enough, then approach the task creatively: my colleagues and I did this and, since we generally work either from home or from our clients' offices, a creative solution for most of us is to have mobile phones and lap top or notebook computers plus a powerful personal computer at home. We also make use of electronic mail (E-mail) systems to keep in touch with each other and, more and more frequently, with our clients. Another absolute must for us is a fax machine/telephone answering machine. For most part, however, you are likely to find that certain basic tools and equipment and a working environment are supplied, but do not let this restrict you in seeking to make your people more effective through the use of modern technology and a pleasant working environment.

THE PSYCHOLOGICAL ENVIRONMENT – COMMUNICATION

Environmental impact goes beyond the purely physical – you have to be aware of the impact of the psychological environment which is generated whenever people have to work together. You have to be sensitive to the 'perceptions' that your team has about such things as each other, the goals, the company itself, internal politics, and the market in which they work. Perceptions are very powerful, they are difficult to define and even more difficult to change; because of this, many managers try to ignore them. In the worst case, perceptions translate into an issue of 'morale'.

In many ways, the cure is a healthy dose of motivation; but why does morale decline?

In almost all the cases I have ever dealt with, the primary cause of a decline in morale – of a negative psychological environment – has been **poor communications**. Some people see information as power and try to restrict its distribution. Some managers distribute all information even when it is not appropriate. Head office staff issue new policies without testing to see if they can be understood. Rumours flash round the company grapevine and are seldom confirmed or denied, thus giving rise to more rumours. Senior management try to hide bad corporate news from their staff only to have it leak out via the press and market, leaving the employees unprepared for the fallout. All these are examples of poor communication, some unintentional, some just plain careless, and all avoidable with a little thought.

So what should you do to ensure good communication for your team? (Here we are dealing with *processes* of communication, rather than style of communication, which is covered in Chapter 3.)

Research carried out by Learning International, an international training company, concluded that one of the key roles of a manager is that of Communicator and ranked it as one of the three most important activities a manager can undertake (along with Strategist – the planning role, and Mentor – the development role). Given that no business can function without communication, the role of communicator is pivotal to the success of the organisation.

So why do so many companies suffer from bad communications if the communicator role is so important? The answer can be found within a combination of certain 'laws of organisational behaviour' or, as Michael Dixon of the *Financial Times* calls them, 'laws of organisational stupidity'. The first of these is:

The Peter Principle – This famous 'law' states that all managers will eventually be promoted to a position which they are not competent to fulfil. Once they have reached such a position, they are no longer really competent to make the decisions that are their responsibility and, since the result of an incorrect decision may cause damage to their career or even their ability to hold onto their job, when faced with a difficult decision they 'pass the buck' to someone else or they avoid making the decision and then cover up their failure to act. This gives rise to what Harvard Professor Chris Argyris calls his Archetype law.

Argyris's Archetype – The more threatening a problem to those responsible for solving it, the deeper it will become ingrained under ramifying layers of camouflage. Once this law has come into effect the whole subject of the decision becomes 'undiscussable' and this eventually leads people to deny the subject exists – at which point communication ceases, the decision is never made, and those responsible become preoccupied by the need to avoid making mistakes. This then leads to what Michael Dixon has called Kelly's Katabolism (a faulty life-support system that kills the organism affected).

Kelly's Katabolism – Errors breed as concentration on avoiding them increases. This next stage in the paralysis of corporate communication then becomes obvious – managers get together in meetings to make decisions but, in an effort to avoid making mistakes, they focus on small items and allow major decisions to go through 'on the nod'. This gives rise to what Professor Jerry Harvey called the Abilene Paradox.

Harvey's Abilene Paradox – People in groups agree on decisions which, as individuals, they know to be stupid. Managers caught in this paradox can always claim that the group agreed to the decision and that no one person was responsible. However, by this stage the whole process of good communication has ceased and those in more junior positions directly affected by the breakdown in communication are left wondering how they can do their job. This leads directly to a lowering of morale and to negative perceptions amongst the workforce.

Once a negative perception about the organisation has

become pervasive among the staff, it shows up in their attitude towards each other and towards their customers and the downward spiral has started. Service quality deteriorates, buck-passing proliferates, sales decline, staff unrest builds, costs increase, profits decline and, in the worst cases, the company is unable to continue trading.

The current trend towards de-layering of middle management and towards empowerment is, I believe, a reaction to this destructive cycle since it is middle management who are most prone to buck-passing and are most likely to be caught up in the process I have just described.

So let us go back to the question: What can you do to improve the communication system for your team? To answer this we need to recognise there are two aspects to communication:

- what has to be communicated, and
- the way it is communicated.

What has to be communicated, and to whom

In today's business environment there are literally hundreds of pieces of information which cross our desks each day and thousands of pieces of information which flow through the organisation and may well affect us and our team. Your first task is to sort this information into what is relevant and what is irrelevant. This is not as easy as you may first think – something that seems irrelevant now may be important later on but you cannot afford to spend too much time filing and indexing information for future retrieval. You must, therefore, develop a system based on a simple precept: there is information which you **know** and there is information which you **know where to find**.

All information can be filed according to this system. The information you know is the information you *need* to do your job and that your team *needs* to do their job. All other information should be filed under the heading of 'know where to find'.

So what is the information you need to know? Essentially, this is the information that directly impacts on the way you do your job **today** or may impact on it within, say, **one month**. This includes items on pricing, market conditions, the competition, company policy, the performance of the company, of the division and of your team.

All other information is available through known sources such as other departments, market research, newspapers, the MIS (Management Information System) system, and so on. In this area, your job is to know who to turn to when you need a piece of information.

Once you have identified the information that is relevant and that you need to know, or your team needs to know, you still have to decide if the format of that information is suitable for dissemination to your team – after all, if they are doing their job properly they will not have time to spend wading through huge quantities of information on the basis that it **may** be useful. The performance-orientated manager will review the information, prepare a digest of it, and put out a **summary sheet** for his team – the summary sheet will also identify the source of the information so that interested team members can request more detailed data.

But let us not forget that you must also keep others supplied with information – for example, your manager, colleagues in related teams or departments, specialist departments, and so on. You need to keep them informed so that they can do their job better and thus allow you to do yours with greater efficiency. Again, the performance-orientated manager will prepare **a digest of relevant information** for circulation upwards and horizontally within the organisation – this information is likely to be very different from that circulated to their team.

Finally, we must also ensure that our clients receive relevant information as this assists in maintaining a good relationship and can significantly reduce the amount of effort required to generate repeat business. In this area, you should co-opt the assistance of the marketing department.

Information and power

Some managers equate having information with having power, and to enhance their power they withhold the information they have from those who need it. This attitude by the manager can and generally does have a serious impact on the morale of their team. One example of this occurred in a large company for which I worked. The department concerned had eight people in it all working in an open-plan office; the manager had a separate office and would frequently call one or two of the team in for a private meeting behind a closed door without informing the others of the subject. The rest of the team then felt excluded, especially if, as a result of the meeting, they were then supposed to be involved in the project. You should always try to ensure that everyone involved in a project is kept informed and you should be sensitive to the effect on morale of withholding information. Managers who do withhold information generally justify their actions by such expressions as 'the information is too sensitive for general distribution' or 'it would be better if only a few of us know about this'. This is clearly very dangerous in terms of the environment within the organisation and in terms of the effectiveness and performance of the people who need access to the information.

While it is very true that certain information should be restricted for sound commercial reasons, it should *never* be withheld from those who need it to do their job effectively. So how do you decide whether to distribute information or withhold it? The basic criteria you should use are:

- does anyone in my team or among the management above me require this information to do their job? and
- what will be the result on the team's effectiveness or morale if this information is withheld?

In this way it will soon become clear if you are withholding relevant information from those who need it: quite simply those people cease to perform as well as they should.

While having knowledge can give you power, misusing that knowledge or information or withholding it from those who need it is damaging to your real power: it is dangerous both in terms of your credibility as a manager and in terms of your ability to lead your team to deliver an enhanced performance.

The way information is communicated

The way information is communicated is governed by the content and quantity. The more complex the subject, the greater the need to allow people to review the material more than once and this means it should be presented in a written format with diagrams whenever appropriate. The use of video and audio presentations is sometimes effective but most companies have not yet come to grips with distributing information this way, and many offices lack the facilities to play back such material. Similarly, if there is a great deal of information that needs to be made available then again the written form is ideal. Most general information (the type that is in the information digest) should be printed and circulated. Many large companies make use of electronic mail systems and this is a good way of transmitting written information quickly to a widespread group of people. Other sorts of information should be delivered face-to-face in team meetings and in one-to-one meetings with individuals. The presentation of the team's business results and the outlining of future plans are examples of information that should be presented in team meetings while conveying information about individual results and future job prospects are better done one-to-one.

In terms of the general written information for your team, the most effective way is to print up the digest and hand-deliver it yourself. This gives a number of benefits:

- you are seen to be interested in distributing information

- you can spend a few minutes with each of your team members – something that can be very motivating for them
- informal contact of this sort allows you to 'keep your finger on the pulse' of the team.

The style you use is also very important. Do you use a formal style, an informal style, bullet points, long descriptive paragraphs, or what? You can refer back to Chapter 3 for guidance on styles of communication. Remember too that, in face-to-face situations, 75–80 per cent of all communication is non-verbal body language – the gestures you use, the way you stand and move, the way and frequency with which you look at the listener – and you should improve your understanding of this very important area by reading some of the books on the subject which I have given in the Reading List.

SUMMARY POINTS

- The physical environment in which you and your team work directly affects everyone's morale and, consequently, their performance.
- The psychological environment (perceptions about the company, the market, colleagues) also affects morale and performance.
- A negative psychological environment is generally caused by poor communications or a complete breakdown in the communications within the organisation.
- The role of Communicator is one of the most important, if not the most important, that you, as a manager, must fulfil.
- Poor communications tend to derive from the 'laws of organisational stupidity'.

- To be a good communicator you need to recognise the two aspects of communication – (i) what has to be communicated, and (ii) the way it is communicated.

- All relevant information must reach all those who need it in a form that they can understand and absorb – this applies to information you communicate to your team and to your senior managers and colleagues.

- Information and power are *not* the same thing and managers who withhold relevant information are damaging themselves, their team, and their company.

9

Cause, Commitment and Goals

'Cause' – what we believe in around here • *the importance of causes* • *corporate causes* • *cause as Mission Statement* • *how is commitment obtained?* • *goals as personal objectives* • *why are goals important?* • *'Smart' goals* • *a goal-setting model* • *goals to enhance performance*

'CAUSE' – WHAT WE BELIEVE IN AROUND HERE

OVER THE YEARS leaders have tried a wide variety of methods to obtain commitment to achievement – most have failed to some extent since they were asking their people to achieve the leader's objective and not their own objective. However, those leaders who have obtained their people's commitment to a goal have done so by establishing the goal as one which their people believe in.

For example, Churchill and Hitler both obtained total commitment from their people to fight the Second World War because each nation's objective became a 'common cause' to which they could adhere. In the simplest terms, in the case of the British, their cause was 'for King and Country' and 'defence of the realm'; the Germans' cause was 'the greater

Fatherland'. The Vietnam war is also an interesting example: for the North Vietnamese their cause was to free their country of colonial occupiers and their corrupt followers and to establish a Communist paradise, a cause for which they fought with courage and tenacity using little in the way of 'hi-tech' weaponry – and they won. The American soldiers, on the other hand, had no real reason for fighting alongside the South Vietnamese, although they had as much 'hi-tech' weaponry and firepower as anyone could want – the cause belonged to the politicians in Washington and not to the American people; as a result, the USA was beaten. Fighting Communism in a far-off country was a cause that the American people could not commit to, and there was huge resentment at the deaths and injuries suffered by their friends and family members drafted into the war.

When people commit to a cause they believe in, they will literally move heaven and earth to achieve their objectives – in some cases, they will even give up their lives. While I am not suggesting that you should be looking for your people to make quite such an heroic sacrifice, to establish a 'common cause' for everyone to work for is something you can and should do.

Some examples of organisational causes:

- to be the biggest software supplier in the world (Microsoft – they are)

- to put a man on the moon by the end of the 1960s (Kennedy's cause for the NASA team – they did)

- to never compromise on quality (Marks & Spencer – they don't)

THE IMPORTANCE OF CAUSES

One of the principal benefits that derives from a common cause is that people feel they **belong**, that what they are doing is important to the success of the enterprise. This, in itself, is highly motivational. And a motivated workforce is something all managers need if the goals and objectives of the team are to be achieved.

An illustration: late one evening in the mid 1960s a visitor to the headquarters of NASA, the US National Aeronautics and Space Administration, came across a man sweeping the corridor. When asked what he was doing, the man replied, 'I'm helping put a man on the moon.'

Another illustration: a group of workers in a factory making electric light bulbs in the US were made the subject of a study and one week were told that as a result of their work performance they could take an extra half hour for lunch for the whole of that week. Their performance (measured in terms of output) did not decline as expected but increased. The following week they were told to take a two-hour lunch break – again their performance increased. In the third week the lunch break was reduced to half an hour – again their performance increased. In the fourth week they were asked to work through without a lunch break – again their performance increased. When asked why, the group replied that they felt they were part of a special project team and the variable lunch break was obviously necessary for the group to hit its objectives.

What both these examples illustrate is that having and believing in a common cause makes people feel they belong and that **group-belonging motivates**.

CORPORATE CAUSES

It is a common assumption that when people join an organisation they do so because they automatically identify with the cause – the objectives of the organisation. After all, if they do not believe in what the organisation is trying to achieve, why do they join? This is, of course, based on a second assumption: that people joining an organisation *know* what the organisation is trying to achieve.

But is this true?

Most people have only a very vague idea of the real objectives of the corporation they work for: most have probably joined 'because it's a good company to work for' – or so they have been told; or 'because I have to earn a living'; or even 'because I didn't know what else to do'. Few have ever really examined what the corporation stands for and is trying to achieve – some may be lucky enough to find out, others may never really know.

If they never really know, can they be expected to deliver the real commitment and performance you, as their manager, want from them? To overcome this handicap, you should ensure that each member of your team knows and understands the objectives of the organisation and that they fully support those objectives – that they become committed to 'the cause'.

CAUSE AS MISSION STATEMENT

In modern business jargon the 'cause' is contained within the 'Mission Statement' – a clearly defined and unequivocal statement of the objectives of the company. But mission statements are not confined to large companies, they are also applicable to single departments, sales teams, office units, and so on. As a manager and leader you must, therefore, think about, develop, and write down a clear and concise statement of the objectives of your team.

There will always be sceptics about the value of mission statements and some recent business books have begun to question the whole idea, but in so doing they are missing the essential point: the mission statement is a clear definition of where we are going and what we are going to achieve, not in terms of our daily, monthly, or annual goals, but in terms of what we want to be. As a Rabbi said to me once, 'If you don't know where you are going, how you will recognise when you have arrived at your destination; your business goals are milestones along the way of the longer journey.'

Some DOs and DON'Ts of mission statements:

DO:

- make it very precise
- make it short
- use simple language
- be realistic but challenging

DON'T:

- be vague
- be all-encompassing
- tell how it is to be achieved

Once the mission statement is ready, *you* must believe in it totally – it is this total belief that will attract the commitment of your team. You must also ensure that everything you and your team do can be fully justified if examined in the light of the mission statement – in this way you can ensure that you and your team are moving towards your goals.

As an example, the following mission statement was contained in the 1994 business plan of one of my clients:

- To be, by 1998, the off-shore financial and investment consultancy-of-choice for upscale individuals in the [...] market by supplying a full range of financial advisory and consultancy services through six offices located in selected geographical locations; and
- To be seen as the prime professional service company in the field by potential consultants and the product suppliers.

Another company had the following mission statement:

- To be the prime supplier of specialty [...] products to at least 1500 clients in [...] by the end of 1994; and
- To be recognised throughout the [...] industry in [...] as the prime source of reference analysis on the complete range of specialty [...] products available.

How is commitment obtained?

The first step is the mission statement – the cause. It must be something in which *you* believe implicitly and explicitly, and it must be believable to others. It is wise, therefore, that, having written a mission statement, you should test it by asking your colleagues how they feel about it, whether they could 'get behind it', whether it could be improved.

Then it has to be **sold** to the team. One thing is for certain, a cause cannot be imposed. You cannot expect commitment if the mission statement is communicated from on high by memorandum or by pinning it on the noticeboard – you have to mount an active sales and marketing effort to discuss the mission statement with your team and to obtain their agreement to it.

A possible approach:

(i) Hold a meeting with your team and explain what you believe the group is trying to achieve – including the goals and objectives.

(ii) Having conceptualised this as a mission statement, read through the statement with them.

(iii) Discuss it with them, be willing to change the phrasing of the mission statement.

(iv) Obtain their agreement on the mission statement for the group.

(v) Encourage everyone to sign the mission statement.

(vi) Provide everyone with a copy of the mission statement printed on a card the size of a credit card.

(vii) Put a copy on the noticeboard and also display it at other prominent points in the office.

(viii) Ask (or require) that all reports (written and oral) reflect what has been achieved in terms of the mission statement.

(ix) Run all meetings around the achievement of the stated mission.

(x) When discussing individual goals and responsibilities, always do so in terms of the contribution they will make towards the team goals and the mission.

(xi) Talk about the team's mission (and mission statement) constantly.

(This is based on the idea that if we repeat something enough times we come to believe it – and so will others.) This constant reinforcement of the mission statement builds commitment within the group so that the team goals and objectives become the overall goal for each member of the team – this is the first step in motivation: getting others to want what we want.

Goals as personal objectives

With the mission statement firmly in place, the team knows what it is trying to achieve, what its objective is. The next step is to get them to understand what they have to do, in terms of activity and performance, for the team to achieve its objective. This, of course, has two distinct aspects – what the team has to achieve, and what the individual has to achieve as part of that team achievement.

In the 1980s psychologists concluded that humans 'are natural goal-achieving organisms' who will strive to achieve any goal they set themselves and in which they believe. They also concluded that any goal imposed from outside (i.e. by another person) was valueless and had no benefit.

Our goals are important to us. Whether a goal is as simple as having a good day or as complex as climbing Mount Everest, we will strive to achieve it and the more we desire to achieve the greater the dedication, the greater the commitment, and the greater the likelihood of success.

Any study of 'success' that you read will show you that the successful person has short- and medium-team goals that build towards their long-term goals; and that achieving each goal in its turn ensures the achievement of the long-term goal of being successful. Furthermore, people who achieve success this way have built a firm foundation for future success and for future happiness.

In terms of performance management, it is vital that you work towards ensuring that the goals of your people build towards the goal that you have to achieve on behalf of the corporation. But, no matter what the pressures from the corporation, you have to remember that your people will have true commitment only to the achievement of their *own* goals. Because *goals are personal objectives*.

WHY ARE GOALS IMPORTANT?

In Chapter 7 you read that if someone is to be motivated they need to have a goal, something to strive for, something they can achieve. And this goal must be something they really want to achieve because the achievement will provide a psychological or material benefit – which is why people do things in the first place.

The problem facing us, as managers, is that many of our team have little real interest in the success of the corporation as an entity because its very size makes identification with corporate goals almost impossible. But identification with corporate goals is vital if you are to succeed – your job, therefore, is to enable your team to connect with corporate goals by breaking them down into team-sized objectives. Once this is done you must persuade your team to 'get behind' the team goals and you do this via your team's mission statement and by focusing all communications in terms of achieving the team goals.

Because team 'belonging' is motivational you have to focus on team-building activities, you have to mould your team into a functional, interdependent unit that is seeking to achieve a realistic goal. In the modern corporate environment, teamwork and the success of the team is vital and there is little scope for the brilliant and inspired individualist – unless they, too, can work as part of the team.

For your team to achieve its goal, each and every person in that team must know exactly what they have to contribute both in terms of basic skills and performance norms, and also in terms of the additional performance that will make the team succeed. In Chapter 5 we examined the need for Job Specifications in which the minimum performance standards for each job are laid down, establishing a level of performance that, if delivered, should enable the whole team to achieve a good level of performance. Unfortunately, in today's business world an average to good performance is seldom enough – competition is on the increase, markets are contracting, products are becoming generic (i.e. they can be bought anywhere) and the average to good performer is going to have to give way to those who deliver superior performance.

So how do you motivate your team members to deliver a superior performance?

You start with commitment to the team goal, then you clearly define the contribution of each individual, and finally you get them to establish their own, performance-enhancing goals. Goals that they can and will commit to, goals that they will do everything possible to achieve – because the goals will be their own.

Without these goals, motivation will decline and success will be difficult. But exactly what are these goals, in reality?

'SMART' GOALS

A goal can be defined as a specific and desired result of a course of action.

There are certain basic rules that apply to goals. They must be:

- realistic, achievable
- believable
- moderately difficult
- measurable
- short-term

but above all else

- they must be clearly defined.

When setting goals you must also remember that an individual can only accept and commit to a goal which has been:

- set for things that *they* control.

Let me start with this last point.

Control over results

For a goal to have any meaning at all, it has to be the achievable result of a course of action, the major processes of which are controlled by the person whose goal it is.

For example, a salesperson can have goals for business acquired, prospects seen, a specific closing ratio, but cannot have a goal for speed of delivery or the quality of after-sales service, if these are provided entirely by a separate part of the organisation. Equally, the dispatcher can have goals for accuracy of delivery, speed of delivery, condition of the goods, but not the overall quantity shipped (except when it relates to a specific order), the quantity of orders, or for the accuracy of the order docket.

Now let's take a look at the other criteria for goals.

Realistic

A goal must be the realistic result of a course of action. Realistic and achievable in terms of the person's ability, the market conditions (including seasonality), and the resources available.

For example, if an experienced machinist can produce forty widgets per hour it would not be realistic to expect a person new to the job to achieve this level of production until they have been trained and have gained experience. And, if the best performance of the experienced machinist is forty widgets per hour, then we cannot expect him to make eighty per hour without a major change in the machinery.

Believable

The person must believe they can achieve the goal and you, the manager, must believe the person can achieve the goal.

As the manager you know whether the goal is realistic and achievable, but it is possible that your team member does not believe he or she can achieve it. In this all too common situation you will need to spend time on building the person's self-confidence and their belief in their own abilities by pointing out and building on previous performance.

Moderately difficult

The goal must stretch the person so that it is a challenge; in this way the goal becomes motivational. Let's go back to the widget maker: if forty per hour is his normal performance then he could be motivated to achieve, say, forty-five per hour (a little over 10 per cent increase).

Measurable

The goal must have measurable results and there must be measurement and monitoring procedures in place to track performance. If a goal is set with an *observable* result, (rather than a measurable one) then criteria must be established to govern what constitutes achievement of that goal. For example, 'to open twenty new accounts in the next two months' is a measurable goal; on the other hand, 'to maintain a clear-desk policy' is a goal with observable results. We can easily define what constitutes a clear desk and can observe whether our people are achieving that goal.

There is one point that is absolutely vital here: goals must have **objective** results, we cannot set goals for *effort* which is **subjective**. For example, 'to work hard at implementing the plan' is *not a goal* as it is entirely subjective and has no measurable or observable result. On the other hand, 'to implement the plan by the end of July' *is a goal* as it has a measurable or observable result.

Short-term

For a goal to be of any value in terms of motivation or improving performance it should be short-term – research was done on this subject and it was found that **monthly** goals were the most motivational and twelve-month (annual) goals were of almost no value. The research found that the motivational value of any goal declined dramatically after three months for every day beyond that period.

In some businesses – especially those with seasonal cycles – it is very difficult to have realistic measurable goals for one month, and worthless to have them for one year. In these circumstances, I recommend setting all goals for three months.

Clearly defined

Goals must be clearly and precisely defined and must avoid all 'woolly words'. Goals, like minimum performance standards, should have a 'what is to be achieved by when' structure.

Our widget-maker's goal could be defined as follows: 'To produce forty-five widgets per hour, each to be machined to within 0.0001 mm tolerances on all dimensions.' This states the **what** (forty-five widgets, each machined within

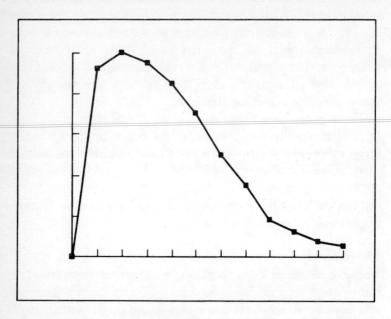

This graph shows the approximate efficiency of goals as a motivational tool against time in months

tolerances) and the **when** (per hour).

There is one other issue worth looking at:

Don't share goals
By sharing of goals, I mean allowing all members of a team to know the goals of all the other members. This is dangerous as it frequently builds resentment and can demotivate very quickly.

The way I have always handled this is to allow the team to know what the team's goal is but not what the individuals' goals are. In this way each person knows everyone has to hit 100 per cent of their individual goal for the team to achieve its goal. This is motivational especially when the individual performances are published in terms of percentage of goal.

Here is a useful mnemonic which helps to summarise most of the above.

Goals must be SMART: **S**pecific
Measurable
Accepted
Realistic
Timely

A GOAL-SETTING MODEL

The process of goal-setting has four stages as far as you are concerned:

(i) determining performance norms for the coming period

(ii) determining past performance of each team member

(iii) private goal-setting interviews

(iv) announcing the new team goal.

Determine the performance norms for the coming period. Obviously, you have to know what you, as the manager, are trying to achieve during the coming period. This means determining the overall objective for the team in general terms and calculating the activity levels needed.

You also have to take into account the seasonal cycle, product launches and marketing programmes likely to have an impact during the period; which of your people will be working during the time, and so on.

With all these factors available you can do a calculation of what each person should be able to achieve.

Determine the past performance of each team member. You need to know what each individual has achieved in the previous period (month or quarter) and, if possible, what they achieved in the same period the previous year.

Hold a private, one-to-one, goal-setting interview with each individual. The individual's goals are a personal commitment between the team member and his manager and should be kept private – at least by the manager.

The goal-setting interview should go something like this:

Step 1: Explain the purpose of the interview

Step 2: Remind of past achievement/performance

Step 3: Ask what they think they can achieve this coming period

Step 4: Guide towards an acceptable (from your point of view) SMART goal

Step 5: Allow them to determine their goal

Step 6: Obtain their commitment to their goal

Step 7: WRITE IT DOWN.

Announce the new team goal. Firstly, add up all the individual volume goals – this makes the team goal. Secondly, check to see if this meets the business goal for the period – if not, review goals with your senior or most mature people. Thirdly, announce the new team goal at the next team meeting – this becomes the **cause** for the period.

GOALS TO ENHANCE PERFORMANCE

Just how much influence do goals have on performance?

This question is one which I have been asked many times over the last few years. Unfortunately, there has been little in the way of reliable research in the business field to quantify the impact of goals, but there is strong anecdotal and observational evidence that just having realistic goals tends to enhance performance by 15 per cent–25 per cent in the short term.

Evidence from other fields of endeavour such as sport and the arts suggests that similar performance enhancement results from having challenging but realistic goals – especially those that step up performance as skills develop.

My own experience suggests that an organisation with no 'goals' for its individual people can achieve an immediate improvement of 20 per cent or more just by having goals – *even if they have not been properly set, and are imposed to a certain extent.* And the experience of success that results from such an improvement allows the individuals to accept that the whole concept of goals and enables the managers to set goals correctly. From this position, it is possible to step up the goals over a period of time, which results in a much improved level of performance.

But how much can goals be stepped up? In theory, it should be possible to improve performance indefinitely, but in reality this is not the case. In a well-run team with properly set minimum performance standards, good development programmes, and properly set goals, it would be normal to look for a 10 per cent increase in any goal over the same goal for the same period in the previous year. However, you must remember to take into consideration the market conditions, the product development cycle (e.g. are the products becoming generic? – if so, performance enhancement may turn to the maintenance of market share), production cycles, changes in pricing and support policies, the marketing programmes, and so on.

If 10 per cent steps are taken each goal cycle, then the overall performance of a team member will improve by 100 per cent over eight to ten goal cycles – i.e. up to 20 per cent improvement in annual performance over two years if you are using quarterly goal cycles. Clearly, such a growth rate in performance cannot be sustained indefinitely but it is surprising how long it can be sustained. The most important point, however, is that the level of performance must be maintained or improved at all times – a decline in performance would indicate a major motivational problem.

If such a major improvement can be obtained through properly set goals, it is clear that goals are vital in the management of your team – but they are only part of the performance story. What good are goals if we cannot see or measure our performance against them – if we have no way of knowing if we are reaching our goals? We will be looking closely at the subject of monitoring and other forms of feedback in the next chapter.

SUMMARY POINTS

- A 'cause' allows everyone to commit themselves to achieving a common goal.
- The cause is defined in a 'mission statement'.
- A common cause gives individuals the feeling of belonging to a group.
- Group-belonging is highly motivational.
- Every working unit should have a mission statement that defines exactly what that unit is trying to achieve.
- The mission statement has to be short and concise.
- To obtain commitment, the mission statement has to be **sold** to the team.
- Goals are vital to an individual's success – all successful people have goals because goals are personal objectives.
- Goals are important for motivation.
- The goals of the individual must reflect the team goals if the individual is to be motivated to achieve the corporate objectives.
- Goals are the specific and desired result of a course of

action.

- Goals must be SMART (Specific, Measurable, Accepted, Realistic, Timely) and they must be for objective results and not subjective ones.

- The process of goal setting has four stages: determine the performance norms for the coming period, determine the past performance of each team member, hold a one-to-one goal-setting interview with each person, summarise the goals and announce the new team goal.

- Goals can enhance performance by 15 per cent–25 per cent.

- Goals should be increased by 10 per cent each time they are set.

10

Feedback: Seeing How We are Doing

The value of feedback • monitoring and recognition • monitoring for motivation • the team or sales meeting • objectives of team meetings • format – agenda • team meeting DOs and DON'Ts • positive feedback • corrective feedback • performance reviews

THE VALUE OF FEEDBACK

WE HAVE JUST been looking closely at goals, what they are, why it is important to have them, and we saw that just having goals can improve performance by 15 per cent–25 per cent. But what good are goals if we do not know how we are doing in terms of achieving them? If we cannot see or measure our performance, we have no idea whether the goals are going to be achieved. Clearly, then, we must monitor our performance and that of our team so that each person receives feedback, and from that feedback we can provide the necessary coaching and development along with motivational support.

Research carried out in the UK and in continental Europe by myself and others has indicated that monitoring and recognising performance in a clear, objective, and public manner can improve performance by a further 15 per cent–25 per cent. Blanchard, the author of the One Minute Manager, carrying out research in the USA, has shown that the impact of quality feedback in a one-to-one situation enhances performance by anything up to 70 per cent.

Taken to its logical conclusion, therefore, if we use goals, monitoring, recognition, and quality feedback – in fact, if we use Performance Management – we can enhance our people's performance by 80 per cent–100 per cent over their current performance.

Is this a wild claim? Well, no. These principles have been successfully used in a wide range of companies throughout the UK and USA and have delivered results well within this range. In one financial institution with branches across Europe and the Middle East, I used these principles successfully with the sales team and they resulted in improvements in performance of between 95 per cent and 280 per cent.

So what is feedback, exactly? Feedback is the name we use to describe the process of giving an individual information about their performance. It includes:

- monitoring and recognition
- positive feedback
- corrective feedback
- performance reviews.

MONITORING AND RECOGNITION

The ability to see if goals are being met – of measuring performance – is a vital part of managing performance. Once the goal has been set it is vital that you establish a monitoring process so that progress towards the goal can be seen. This simple and very fundamental step can enhance performance by providing a constant source of motivation and self-correction for your team.

A simple illustration of this is an aeroplane. The pilot has a goal of reaching a cruising altitude of 36,000 feet, so he pulls back the control stick and begins to climb. He knows how fast he is climbing, how far he has climbed, and he knows when he has reached his cruise altitude by looking at the altimeter which measures the height above sea-level and the rate of change in height.

There is a second very important point that this example illustrates: the monitoring process tells the *individual* of his progress towards his goal. The altimeter would be of no benefit to the pilot if it could be seen only by the air traffic controller (manager) – it is the pilot who needs to see the altimeter and to be responsible for measuring his altitude. Knowing where he is in relation to the ground focuses the pilot's attention on staying at the right altitude.

In the same way, you need to establish a simple process of performance monitoring that can be, and is, used by the individuals in your team.

The biggest mistake managers make in this area is to try to measure too many things in too much detail. All this does is distract the individual from the process of achieving their goals and the monitoring becomes an end in itself. Of course, you as a *manager* have to measure a great many things in great detail – but that is your responsibility and should not be delegated to your staff. Instead, you should establish a simple measure of performance for your people – a measure that encompasses all your other requirements.

Experience has shown that when the individual is responsible for monitoring their own performance they tend to be accurate, honest, and up-to-date with their information. They also record that information in a form which they can carry with them – typically, in their diaries or on hand-held electronic organisers.

Monitoring for motivation

Using performance monitoring as a motivational tool is an area that is all too frequently overlooked by managers – to their cost.

The truth is that we all compare ourselves to others in our team or peer group – witness the desire most of us exhibit to know our own examination results and to compare them to those of our class mates, or the way that athletes track their own performance against those of other competitors. This alone can produce performance-enhancing pressures: when a team member is seen to be performing below expectations, other members of the team will assist them or apply peer pressure to obtain an improvement.

To utilise this natural response within your business environment, you combine simplified 'management by objectives' and 'attitude motivation' techniques into a powerful but very, very simple five-step process:

(i)   you ask the individual for his goals

(ii) you add the goals together (where volume goals are being used, as in a sales or production environment)

(iii) you announce the team goals (which become the 'cause' for the period)

(iv) you display the goals on a bar chart and record performance against the goals in terms of a percentage of goal

(v)   at the end of the period you give recognition to those who have achieved their goals.

This process is repeated at the beginning of each goal cycle (i.e. monthly or quarterly).

Let's look at these elements in detail. Remember that the objective is to **motivate** and not to **manipulate**.

Ask the individual. In a **private** interview with each team member in turn, and following the goal-setting model outlined in the previous chapter, agree the individual's goal for the coming period.

Add the goals together. The summation of the individually

agreed volume goals make up the team goal. The team must *know* that the team goal is the summation of the individually agreed goals and *not* something imposed by senior management. (Obviously this summation must be guided during the goal-setting process so that it meets the required objective – if necessary you may need to revisit some of the goals.)

Announce the team goals. You must announce the team goal during a team meeting so that everyone knows what the team is trying to achieve during the coming period. Since success as a team depends on everyone achieving their goals, the team goal becomes the 'cause' for the period.

Display the goals. Display performance, in terms of **percentage of individual goal,** on a prominently positioned bar chart. Using this approach ensures that even the person with the lowest goals is made to feel part of the team. Everyone realises that his or her contribution makes up the team goal and that the team will fail if any individual fails to deliver 100 per cent of goal.

The key here is that the display *must be in terms of percentage of goal* and not in absolute volume terms because top performers will normally deliver higher goals than those new to the job and absolute volumes can demotivate the newcomers.

This process of displaying the performance against goals can also be used in non-volume environments since everyone should have goals that can be measured (or observed) and thus a percentage performance can be obtained.

It is vital, in terms of team motivation, that **all team members** appear on this chart.

Recognition. Since motivation requires recognition you must recognise good performance at all times – in terms of performance monitoring, this recognition is the public acknowledgement of superior performance.

But you must be careful: you cannot praise a performance

that is below the person's goals except in general terms – what you must do is recognise and praise any person who is above their goal (i.e. in excess of 100 per cent of goal) *and* the top producer irrespective of whether this person is at 100 per cent of his goal or not. This last point is very important in terms of a sales team where a top producer may well deliver more volume than the rest of the team but does have proportionately higher goals.

The time and place for the delivery of this recognition is at a team meeting.

THE TEAM OR SALES MEETING

The Team and/or Sales Meeting is an important activity which underpins performance management within the business environment. The principal purpose of this meeting is to provide feedback and, if done correctly, it is an outstandingly worthwhile and powerful management tool; however, it must be planned carefully.

Team and/or Sales Meetings – run by you as manager and attended by all members of your team – should be held regularly and at a frequency that matches the activity period. For example, if your goal cycle is one month, then there should be a team or sales meeting at the end of each month; if the activity period is quarterly, then the meeting should take place at the end of each quarter.

(The Team or Sales Meeting is not to be confused with the frequent planning/reporting meetings that all good managers hold.)

Objectives of team meetings

The meeting has **five** prime objectives:
1 to deal with administration
2 to carry out simple training
3 to inform

4 to give plans
5 to motivate

Format – agenda

(i) *Welcome*. This should be short and to the point. You welcome them to the meeting, define what the meeting is about, hand out the agenda, and tell them what time the meeting will finish. Introduce any guests you have invited.

(ii) *Handle any obvious negatives (if none, delete this step)*. This is the time to mention anything that may adversely affect the team's motivation so that it can be dealt with cleanly and then the rest of the meeting can rebuild the motivation. Items to be covered may include such things as: people leaving the team, redundancies even if they are in another part of the organisation, poor corporate results, adverse market conditions, major changes in pricing policy, changes in personnel policy, and so on.

It is also the time to deal with the team performance **if this is more than 10 per cent–15 per cent** *below* **goal**. However, it is not a time to 'have a go' at your team – what is past is past and you should address the issue in terms of a performance about which you all (the team and yourself) should be concerned.

Although you should encourage a few questions at this stage, it is not a time for a major discussion and if anybody has a question on a specific point this should be answered at a separate meeting.

(iii) *'HOW TO' simple group training*. A team meeting is not the time to run a major training programme but it is a good time to carry out some simple but important group training such as how to handle a new product or process or how to handle a specific situation. It is a good idea to involve the team in this activity by asking one of them to lead the 'training' session (obviously this person must be invited to do so in good time so that they can prepare properly).

(iv) *Attitude reinforcement*. Obviously, you should seek to reinforce positive attitudes about the business, about the team, and about commitment to the cause. This is the time to involve your guests, especially if they are to talk about the business and the way it is going (if the message is negative, then do not invite a speaker – it is your job to handle negatives earlier in the meeting). If the guest is from outside the company, for example a well known businessman or a motivational speaker, then they can deliver support at this point. A word of warning though, use outside speakers sparingly, as most team members are more interested in listening to people they admire from within the company.

(v) *Give recognition*. This is the central activity of the meeting and the point at which you are delivering the main motivational thrust.

You should first of all comment on specific praiseworthy activity by individual team members: for example, the development of a new marketing approach, the successful handling of a major 'problem', a specific significant sale. Remember, it is important to relate the activity to the team member by name.

Then you should discuss the team performance providing it is on target (or, at least, no more than 10 per cent–15 per cent below target). When the team has had a successful performance, emphasise and praise this by putting it into context and relating it to the difficulties that have had to be overcome and the effort that has had to be made.

Move on to recognising by name those who have achieved 100 per cent or more of their goal – giving their percentage performances – and make particular mention of those who are the highest percentage above goal. It is a very effective motivational tool to ask each person to stand up or come to the front of the meeting at this point – especially if your team is quite large. If your practice is to give rewards for performance, now is the time to do it.

Finally, you should acknowledge your top performers by name and give their actual performance (as against percentage).

If you have time, it is helpful and motivational to ask each of your goal achievers and top performers to comment on their performance and to mention what they have found to be particularly important in reaching their goal.

If you have invited a senior manager, use them to say a few words of congratulations to the top people and to hand out any awards. Encourage photographs to be taken of any presentations.

(vi) *Sell the new team goal, forthcoming events, and close.* Since it is essential that the team leave the room in a motivated frame of mind, this must be a very positive activity. It is the time when the team goal for the new period is announced along with the plans and activities for achieving it. (Obviously, it is important to have carried out the new goal-setting interviews prior to this meeting.) And you must make a major effort to obtain the commitment of the team to the goal.

If you are going to run an incentive programme during this period, or a competition, then this is the time to announce it – along with the prize – and to hand out the rules.

The close is not the time for team discussion; it is your opportunity to send everyone away with a positive message.

Team meeting DOs and DON'Ts

DO change venues. Changing the location of the meeting helps maintain enthusiasm and interest. Many organisations have found it highly motivational to hold the meeting outside the office – in a nearby hotel, for example – although using a conference room or someone else's office is also effective.

DO ensure the meeting takes place in business time. The team meeting is a business activity and should always take place during business hours – the last thing on a Friday is often popular as this allows the team to socialise afterwards. Some organisations like to provide a post-meeting buffet or drink as this has proved to be a good team-building activity.

DO change layout. Ensure that the layout of the room is changed as this avoids the meeting becoming 'routine'. Large teams frequently use a 'lecture' format for practical reasons of space but even this can be varied, a long narrow format alternating with a wide shallow format or even a curved arrangement. Small teams can use a circle or even an arrangement based around individual tables.

Avoid having people sit in long rows behind tables as this creates formal barriers and does not facilitate freedom of movement.

DO check layout and equipment. To ensure that you have an effective meeting, you need to arrive early to check that the room layout is as you want it and that all the equipment you need is ready and working – we have all experienced meetings during which equipment is not working or screens and flipcharts cannot be seen (and, even worse, the colours of the flipchart pens are not legible). It is also worth checking the lighting and heating within the room.

DON'T have a top table. If you need to have a table for your papers and other aids then place the table to one side. You, yourself, should be on your feet most of the meeting and if you must sit then sit amongst your team. Any guests you have invited should also sit amongst the team.

DON'T start late or finish late. Your meetings must always start at the right time and must finish at the time you said. Meetings that start late or overrun generate a disproportionate amount of demotivation which defeats the object of the meeting.

DON'T have A.O.B! The initials A.O.B. stand for Any Other Business. The only business to be discussed at the meeting is that which *you* want discussed – any other subject raised should be handled at a separate meeting.

Monitoring, the public display of goal achievement in percentage terms, and the public recognition of performance are vital to the motivation of our team, but what can be done to maintain and enhance these from day to day? The answer lies in individual feedback designed to recognise good performance and good effort, and enhance future performance by supplying appropriate coaching as and when required – often in an informal situation.

This individual feedback is carried out through three distinct processes: positive feedback, corrective feedback, and performance reviews.

POSITIVE FEEDBACK

People crave praise – they desire it almost above anything else, but only when the praise is deserved, and delivered in a positive, genuine manner and with no 'but' attached. Positive feedback (or praising) is a very powerful tool, but its power is reduced if overused or used inappropriately.

Positive feedback should be used only when actions have produced a result that has helped the individual or team towards their goal. We do not praise effort, we praise results. The key to successful positive feedback is delivering it publicly **as soon as you discover the situation worthy of praise**.

Positive feedback is a three-step process:

(i) specify what was done well

(ii) specify how the performance has made a difference to the individual or the team

(iii) express appreciation of, and confidence in, the improved performance.

WARNING: **Never attach a 'rider' to positive feedback** – i.e. never exhort greater efforts, never add a 'but'.

Used correctly and in a timely manner, positive feedback leaves the individual feeling good about themselves, it motivates, and reinforces the performance.

CORRECTIVE FEEDBACK

Most people have been subjected to so much destructive criticism during their lives that they fear it and will often close their minds to it. But criticism does not have to be destructive, it does not have to be negative, and it can be of great benefit when delivered correctly.

Corrective feedback is used when a person's performance has been good but not quite to the expected or desired standard. It is designed to assist the person correct a small fault in their performance and thus bring it back to the correct standard.

Like positive feedback, corrective feedback should be used informally and as soon as the performance in need of correction is noticed. Unlike positive feedback, it is often better to deliver corrective feedback in a semi-private situation – by this, I do not mean you should call the person away from their desk, but that the conversation should be a private one.

The corrective feedback process has three (possibly, four) steps:

(i) specify what was good about the performance

(ii) specify what should be changed about the performance and how this can be done

(iii) (agree a course of action if necessary)

(iv) express confidence in the person and their ability to deliver the expected performance.

Used correctly, corrective feedback leaves the person feeling good about themselves but aware of the need to improve their performance. It enhances performance and is motivational – in time, it becomes welcome.

PERFORMANCE REVIEWS

Performance reviews should be a regular part of performance management and are an important tool for motivating your team – they have little or nothing to do with the formal Annual Appraisals discussed in Chapter 5. Performance reviews are less formal, should take place whenever a team member has produced a performance **below** or **well above expectations**, but please remember performance reviews are always **non-disciplinary**.

The purpose of a performance review is to determine the cause and reasoning behind someone's actions or performance *before* we use further skills to coach, train, or manage the situation. It is not only used when performance is below expectations, but also when expectations are exceeded by a significant factor – in which case we may be looking at our own goal-setting as much as their results.

The performance review interview is a forum for:

- reviewing progress
- giving feedback
- identifying strengths and weaknesses
- resolving problems
- establishing roles and responsibilities
- defining standards to be achieved
- setting priorities and goals
- identifying training and development needs.

The core skills involved in conducting effective performance reviews are:

- preparation

- structuring the review discussion
- beginning and ending the review discussion
- active listening
- asking questions and probing
- giving feedback.

Let's take these first three skills one by one, and cover the remainder in a model performance review.

Preparation
Before the performance review discussion it is up to you, as the manager, to:

- set your agenda
- collect as much relevant information about the team member as possible and ensure you have all relevant performance data and norms
- prepare the environment and ensure quiet and privacy
- ensure the team member has an opportunity to prepare as well.

Structuring the review discussion
It is vital that the discussion is properly structured by having an agenda as this will help you:

- avoid getting sidetracked and thus risk not covering important issues
- keep the discussion relevant
- guide the interview towards a successful conclusion
- remember what was said
- be professional and feel more confident.

The agenda is only a guideline and not a rigid control. It is also important to be aware that the interviewee is likely to have a personal agenda which needs to be taken into account.

During the performance review it is also up to you, as the interviewer, to:

- define the purpose of the discussion
- set the tone and establish rapport
- guide the discussion
- cover your agenda
- help the interviewee cover their agenda
- set any objectives or plan any further actions
- summarise the key points of the discussion

Beginning and ending the review discussion

Beginnings:

(i) greet the team member by name

(ii) break the ice with a few informal words

(iii) agree the purpose of the performance review and encourage the team member to say what they hope to get out of it

(iv) outline the form the review will take.

All these are essential for establishing rapport and trust and ensuring cooperation.

Endings:

(i) ask if there are any questions the team member would like to ask

(ii) summarise the main points raised in the review discussion and check to see if the team member agrees

(iii) agree a further plan of action

(iv) close the performance review with thanks and an expression of confidence.

Performance reviews – a model

Step 1: **Position** – see *Beginnings*, above. 'Position' the interview by stating the purpose of the performance review.

Step 2: **Background** – describe the current versus the expected performance. Identify what was good about the current performance.

Step 3: **Probe** – ask questions in a non-judgemental way to find out the reasons and cause of the performance under review. Listen actively.

Step 4: **Confirm** – you need to confirm your understanding of the response without accepting or rejecting it. This is done by summarising what you have been told by the person, using their words as much as possible.

Step 5: **Check** – check back with the person that your understanding is correct.

Step 6: **Explore** – invite solutions and/or offer suggestions. Select the best alternatives.

Step 7: **Action** – develop a course of action to bring performance in line with expectations (or goals). Of course, if the performance is better than expected, then the next step is to re-evaluate the goals and bring them into line with the performance and to evaluate it.

Step 8: **Conclude** – see *Endings*, above. Conclude the interview, expressing confidence in the person.

Remember: they should talk and you should listen.

SUMMARY POINTS

- Just having goals can increase performance by 15 per cent–25 per cent but quality feedback can improve performance by a further 70 per cent.

- Feedback comprises four activities: monitoring and recognition, positive feedback, corrective feedback, and performance reviews.

- Monitoring allows each individual to see how they are progressing against their own goals and how others are progressing against their goals.

- Monitoring should always be displayed in terms of percentage of goal – this is motivational.

- You should monitor and display only the key activities and key goals.

- Monitoring for motivation is a five-step process: ask the individual for their goals, add the goals together, announce the new team goal, display the goals (in percentage terms) on a publicly positioned bar chart, and at the end of the period provide recognition of above-goal performance.

- Hold regular team or sales meetings – at the end of each period for which goals have been established (monthly or quarterly).

- Team or sales meetings have a fixed agenda and only those items on the agenda can be discussed.

- Start and finish all meetings on time.

- Always make a public display of recognising above-goal performance and the top producers.

- Provide positive feedback to an individual as soon as you discover a situation worthy of praise.

- Positive feedback is a three-step process: specify what was done well, specify how it has made a difference to the individual or team, and express your appreciation of the improved performance.

- *Never* ask for additional effort when giving positive feedback – doing so diminishes the value of the praise.

- Give corrective feedback when you discover a good performance that could be improved by a slight change in approach or attitude.

- The corrective feedback process has three (or four) steps: specify what was good about the performance, specify what should be changed to improve the performance, (agree a course of action, if necessary,) and express your confidence in the person's ability to deliver the improved performance.

- Performance reviews should be a regular part of your management activities and should take place whenever a performance is *below* or *well above* the desired standard.

- Performance reviews are held in private and are *non-disciplinary*.

- The keys to performance reviews are preparation, structure, and good listening skills.

- There are eight steps in a performance review: position the interview, provide the background, ask questions about the performance, confirm your understanding, check that your understanding is correct, explore solutions, establish an action plan, conclude by expressing confidence in the person.

11
Where Do You Go From Here?

AS I MENTIONED in the Introduction, the techniques and skills outlined in this book can help you achieve outstanding results. Putting them into practice takes time and commitment and you cannot expect instant improvements. But you have to start somewhere. So, where should you begin?

My favourite starting point is with goal-setting (Chapter 9) and the monitoring and display of performance (Chapter 10). This can be introduced easily and without too much trouble. Remember to tell everyone what you are doing and, as a first step, ask them for their goals and just write them down. To begin with, don't try to calculate what they should be doing as this will seem threatening. Put their goals up on the chart and record their performance. Don't make a big deal over it, just do it and watch the result. In almost all the cases I have been involved in (and that have been reported to me) the result is remarkable – the team members are, at first, sceptical and try to show they are not interested. After a week or two everyone is looking at the board and after a couple of months they will check the board regularly and will soon tell you when you have failed to update the information.

At this point you can start introducing the full goal-setting and monitoring process, followed by the team meetings. The next stage is to introduce the rest of the feedback techniques, covered in Chapter 10.

The improved performance and motivation of your team

will then allow you to bring in all the rest of the performance management techniques.

Of course, you will have been using your time wisely and will be following up on your own development (Chapter 3: time management and so on) and will also have begun developing the Job Specifications and Profiles (Chapter 5) which you will introduce over time.

To introduce the whole process takes around three to six months of concentrated effort but the results are worth it.

Take your time, don't rush it, and you will soon be able to say that you really are a Performance Manager.

Select Reading List

I am frequently asked for a reading list of useful books on management and selling – the selection of books in print on these two subjects is enormous and growing weekly and any list will contain only a small proportion of the best; this selection contains some that I have found the most useful, accessible, and classic.

I General background reading

I'm OK – You're OK, Thomas A. Harris (Pan Paperback 1973)
A rather heavy but interesting book on Transactional Analysis (or, how we act towards another person determines how they act towards us). A basic textbook on human psychology.

Six Thinking Hats, Edward de Bono (HarperCollins 1989)
Six Action Shoes, Edward de Bono (HarperCollins 1991)
The lateral thinker at his best – modern commentators are claiming that these two books are set to become the most influential books in the field. Some have found it hard to work with the analogies and approach (which I suspect are designed to break the mindset of the modern manager) but they are well worth the effort.

Think and Grow Rich, Napoleon Hill (Fawcett 1979)
The Magic of Thinking Big, David J. Schwartz (Pocket Books, 1995)
The Power of Positive Thinking, Norman V. Peale (Cedar 1988)
These three are the 'original' books on positive thinking and date from 1937 to the early 1960s. They are still extremely relevant and are the foundation for most of the later books on the same subject. Good personal development material.

The Official Guide to Success, Tom Hopkins (Granada 1985)
A very readable derivative of Peale's *The Power of Positive Thinking*, written by an extremely talented and successful salesman turned

consultant. Despite its title, it is a serious book that builds, in a modern way, on the previous three books listed here.

The Art of War, Sun Tzu (trans. S. B. Griffith, for Oxford Paperbacks 1971)
This 2,500-year-old classic of military strategy is the 'bible' for most senior managers in Japan and Asia (despite being written by a Chinese general) – the strategic thinking is as relevant today as it was 2,500 years ago. Famous western generals such as Wellington, Napoleon, Rommel, Montgomery, de Gaulle, Eisenhower, and MacArthur have all acknowledged their debt to Sun Tzu as have the CEOs of Toshiba, Sony, Mitsubishi, Honda, and others. This version is very readable and easy to understand.

A Book of Five Rings, Miyamoto Musashi (Fontana 1984)
Written in 1645 by a Japanese Samurai who was a Master of Kendo (swordsmanship), this book, like Sun Tzu's *The Art of War*, acts as a 'bible' for most senior managers in the Far East. The strategies outlined by Miyamoto Musashi are more than relevant in today's world.

The New Realities, Peter Drucker (Mandarin 1990)
Drucker is *the* management guru in the West. A Hungarian working in the USA, he is the author of numerous interesting, useful, and readable books on management. This one takes a good look at the world of the 1990s in terms of society and commerce in particular. Essential reading if you want to understand the new themes.

The Empty Raincoat, Charles Handy (Hutchinson 1994)
This and all others by Handy are a must. In many ways, Handy is the new management guru – a natural successor to Drucker. Handy has a major advantage over most gurus – he has actually been a senior manager in a major company.

In Search of Excellence, Tom Peters and Robert Waterman (HarperCollins, 1995)
The first shot in the Service Quality campaign as Peters and Waterman try to show how and why adding value through service excellence is the key to future business success.

A Passion for Excellence, Tom Peters and Nancy Austin (Fontana, 1986)
The follow-up (after five years) to *In Search of Excellence* in which

Peters and Austin try to identify how things went right or wrong for the subjects of many of Peters' previous studies – conclusion: we must continually seek to improve the service (thus adding value) as there is no such thing as a definitive level of service excellence.

Thriving on Chaos, Tom Peters (Macmillan, 1988)
A compulsively readable look at business in the late 1980s and why some companies are moving forward and others are losing ground. If you care for the company you work for, you should be a disciple of Peters.

Liberation Management, Tom Peters (Macmillan, 1992)
Again, compulsively readable. This time Peters takes the argument one stage further and focuses on the successful strategies needed for the 1990s: (a) involve your customers in your products and services, (b) work in project teams in 'flat' organizations, (c) add value (yet again) by offering products that fit fashionized (*sic*) specialized opportunities, (d) empower your people to get the job done (most will be very responsible about costs and will make the company even more money), and finally (e) don't stand still or a competitor will overtake you.

Making it Happen, John Harvey-Jones (Collins 1988)
A management autobiography by the ex-chairman of ICI, the UK chemicals giant. Gives a great deal of insight to how a successful business leader thinks.

II Understanding business

There are dozens of books in this category but my all-time favourite is:
The Genghis Khan Guide to Business, Brian Warnes (Osmosis 1984)
This book was written by the then head of Midland Bank Venture Capital Ltd. The subject matter is a clear, non-technical, look at the financial side of managing a business and is a *must* for anyone who either hopes to run a business successfully or wants to go into Financial Control.

The Genghis Khan Guide to Business – Cash Flow Handbook, also by Warnes (Osmosis 1985), is a companion to *The Genghis Khan Guide to Business*. It can be read separately although it makes more sense when you have read the main book first.

III Management development

Again, there are literally dozens of good books – I have picked the six which could form the nucleus of a collection.

The One Minute Manager, Kenneth Blanchard and Spencer Johnson (Fontana 1983)
Putting the One Minute Manager to Work, Kenneth Blanchard and Robert Lorber (Fontana 1983)
These two books, which take the parable form, look at how we can motivate and develop our teams by improving our coaching, communication, and general understanding of the psychology of the relationship between manager and staff.

The One Minute Manager Meets the Monkey, Kenneth Blanchard, William Oncken and Hal Burrows (Fontana, 1991)
'Don't take on the problem if the problem isn't yours. That monkey doesn't belong to you.' Quite the best of the bunch, it is essentially a guide to improving your control over your time so that you really deal with the priorities. Useful for managing upwards, sideways, and downwards.

The Power of Ethical Management, Kenneth Blanchard and Norman V. Peale (Cedar 1988)
Subtitled 'You don't have to cheat to win', this book deals with personal ethics in a management situation – should be essential reading for all managers who want to be able to look themselves in the eye and tell themselves they have done the right thing.

The Zen Way to Be an Effective Manager, Radha (Mercury 1991)
A challenging book that brings Eastern thinking to Western management in a practical, useful, and readable manner – definitely not heavy but it does require the reader to think.

Managerial Effectiveness, William Reddin (McGraw Hill)
A clear, thoughtful, study of 'situational management'. The basis of the theory is that all situations and people need to be managed differently if the 'best' result is to be achieved. Reddin makes the case that all managers must be highly flexible in their management style if they are to be effective managers in a wide range of situations. A little heavy in places but easily understood and extremely valuable.

Leadership Secrets of Attila the Hun, Wess Roberts (Bantam 1989)
Victory Secrets of Attila the Hun, Wess Roberts (Bantam 1993)
Written with humour and insight, these books tackle the subject of leadership and especially the principles and areas of concern that have long served those having the will to lead.

IV Communication

People Skills, Dr Robert Bolton (Prentice Hall 1979)
Widely acknowledged as just about the best book on effective communication. This is not a book just for managers – it is a book for anyone and everyone who would like to communicate better with people around them (at home, at work, socially). It covers active listening, non-verbal messages, assertion, conflict management, and problem solving. This book is a *must* in anybody's collection.

The Secret Language of Success, Dr David Lewis (Corgi 1990)
Probably the best book on the subject of body language (or, more correctly, Non-verbal Communication). Many people have ignored this subject, but, with 75 per cent or more of communication taking place silently, we ignore it at our peril. This book looks at what it is and how to use it.

Body Language, Dr Joseph Braysich (Braysich Enterprises 1979)
A more catchy attempt at the same thing. Illustrated and very easy to read but less thoughtful.

V Selling

There are literally thousands of books on the subject – most of them repeating the same thing over and over again. Many books even attempt to tell you that, if you follow their method you will be guaranteed success. The following books are a good starting point.

How to Master the Art of Selling, Tom Hopkins (Grafton 1983)
A practical, hands-on approach, Hopkins conveys the methods and process behind being a successful salesperson (and he was one of the best). He covers things like time management, prospecting methods, handling the sales interview, closing, and personal development.

Everything is Negotiable, Gavin Kennedy (Arrow 1984)
Negotiation is the opposite of selling. In selling we find out what the

prospect wants and match it with one of our products or services; in negotiation we find out all his objections to our offer and we trade off, balancing what we offer him with what he offers us. This book covers the subject in easily understood language.

VI Miscellaneous

Getting Things Done, Roger Black (Michael Joseph 1987)
A radical new approach to managing time and achieving more at work – perhaps the best of the time-management books.

Total Quality Management, John S. Oakland (Butterworth Heinemann 1989)
The most influential of the TQM practitioners – this book is a 'bible' on the subject and a prerequisite for the implementation of a TQM programme, but it is not easy reading.

Re-engineering the Corporation, Michael Hammer and James Champy (Nicholas Brearley 1993)
The original book on the subject and one of the easiest to understand. However, it does not contain their latest 'warning' – that of all re-engineering projects undertaken a full 80 per cent fail because of lack of commitment at the very top. Re-engineering is not an easy option and it can be very painful and traumatic.

VII Psychometric Profiles

Personal Time Profile, Sandy Ellvers-Dix (LPT Productions)
Personal Leadership Profile, Sandy Ellvers-Dix (LPT Productions)
Personal Behaviour Profile, Sandy Ellvers-Dix (LPT Productions)
These three psychometric profiles, which are included in this book by kind permission of their author, are written by Sandy Ellvers-Dix who runs LPT Productions, a company specialising in profiles and a wide range of management training. For further information about the training services, their range of profiles or to obtain copies for use within your own organisation, please contact Sandy or her partner, Lee Bushby, at LPT Productions, South Inch Business Centre, Shore Road, Perth, Scotland PH2 8BW (Tel: 0738 21189; Fax: 0738 21192).

Index

Abilene paradox, 187
accessibility, offices, 62
accommodating behaviour, 120
action plans, 24-5
Adair, John, 6, 89-90, 123, 124
administrative assistants,
 management contact, 85-6
agendas:
 meetings, 41
 sales meetings, 217-20
aggressive behaviour, 119-20
annual appraisals, 146-50
annual budget meeting, 14-15
appraisals, annual, 146-50
Argyris, Chris, 187
Argyris's archetypes, 187
Ashridge Management College, 123
assertive behaviour, 119
assertiveness, 55-6, 119
 written communications, 67-8
attitude reinforcement, 218-19
avoidance behaviour, 120

belongingness, 173, 195-6, 202
Blanchard, Kenneth, 123
buck-passing, 187, 188

capacity planning, 19-23
career planning, 77-80
causes, 194-9
 corporate, 196-7

 importance of, 195-6
 as a mission statement, 197-9
clear-desk policies, 38-9
clothes, personal image, 62-5
coaching, 158-64
commitment:
 causes and, 194-5
 obtaining, 199-200
communication:
 information, 188-92
 memoranda, 71-4
 psychological environment, 185-92
 spoken, 73-7, 192
 written, 66-73, 192
competitions, motivation and, 177
constraints, defining, 19-23
corporate culture, 125-6
corrective feedback, 222-3
courtesy, visitors, 61
criticism, corrective feedback, 222-3

decisions:
 Abilene paradox, 187
 meetings and, 40
delegation, 39
demotivation, 150
development programme,
 coaching, 161-4

digests of relevant information, 189, 191-2
diplomacy, written communications, 69-70
Dixon, Michael, 186, 187
dress codes, 62-5
Drucker, Peter, 79

electronic mail, 71-4
Ellvers-Dix, Sandy, 43, 122
empowerment, 188
environment, office, 9, 11-12
equipment, 184, 185
    meetings, 221
esteem, incentives, 173

families, 42-3
feedback, 212-28
    corrective, 222-3
    monitoring, 213-17
    performance reviews, 223-9
    positive, 222
    sales meetings, 217-22
    value of, 212-13
fighting fires, 35-6
finance directors, 14
forced ranking, 148-50
foreign nationals, managing, 123-6

goals:
    action plans, 25
    annual budget meetings, 14-15
    believable, 204
    challenge of, 204
    clearly defined, 205-6
    control over results, 203-4
    corporate, 202
    establishing, 9, 10
    feedback, 212-29
    importance of, 201-3
    incompatible with performance, 23-4
    measurable, 204-5
    monitoring, 213-17
    motivation and, 169-72, 175
    performance enhancement, 208-10
    and performance standards, 131-3
    personal development, 77-80
    as personal objectives, 200-1
    private life, 79-80
    realistic, 204
    setting, 207-8
    sharing, 206-7
    short-term, 205
    smart, 203-7
    time management, 52-3
    union cooperation, 124
group training, 218
group-belonging, motivation and, 178

Harvey, Jerry, 187
Harvey's Abilene paradox, 187
human resources, 158, 164-6
    annual appraisals, 146-50
    characteristics profile, 134-41
    coaching, 158-64
    commitment, 199-200
    communication, 185-92
    development, 153-67
    forced ranking, 148-50
    implementing job specifications, 146
    job profiles, 134-41
    job specification, 129-34
    motivation, 168-70
    performance standards, 130, 131-4, 146-50
    reassigning, 143-4
    recruiting, 129, 141-3

training, 144-5

image:
  behaviour, 58-9
  clothes, 62-5
  communication style, 66-77
  manager's office, 58, 59-62
  personal, 57-65
individuals, developing, 6
informality:
  dress codes, 64, 65
  written communications, 70
information:
  communication, 191-2
  power and, 190-1
  sources, 187-9

job profiles, 134-41
job specifications, 129-34
  implementation, 146
Jones, Steve, 10-11
junior managers, management contact, 86-7

Kelly's katabolism, 187

leader, definition, 5-6
leadership:
  foreign nationals, 123-6
  personal leadership profiles, 90-106
Learning International, 186
listening, communication skills, 74-6
lists, using, 37-8

management styles, 9, 10-11, 82-127
  choosing, 83-7
  foreign nationals, 123-6
  personal behaviour profiles, 107-23
  personal leadership profiles, 90-106
  preferred, 88-90
  relationship orientation, 83
  task orientation, 83-4
  team style, 88
management-imposed activities, 34
managers:
  definition, 5
  responsibilities, 6-7
manipulation, 10, 168-70
marketing officers, management contact, 85
Maslow, Abraham, 170-1, 173
measuring performance, 213-17
meetings, 39-42, 217-21
  agendas, 217-20
  location, 60, 220
memoranda, 71-4
minimum performance standards, 131-4, 146-50
  training for, 164-6
mission statements, 197-9
monitoring, 213-17
  action plans, 25
motivation, 9-10, 168-79
  maintenance of, 10
  meetings and, 41
  monitoring for, 214-17

objectiveness, written communications, 68-9
objectives, 14-27
  achieving, 33-4
  defining, 17-18
  personal, 77-80
office environment, 9, 59-62, 183-93
  accessibility, 62
  communication, 185-92
  layout, 59-60

location, 58
physical environment, 183-5
psychological environment, 185-92
visitors, 61
organisation, personal, 32-6

parameters, action plans, 25
participation, motivation and, 177
pay levels:
  incentives, 173
  motivation, 172
people, action plans, 25
performance management, definition, 7-12
performance reviews, 223-7
performance standards, 130, 131-4, 146-50
personal behaviour profile, 107-23
personal development, 31-81
  achieving objectives, 33-4
  assertiveness, 55-6
  balance, 42-3
  being organised, 32-6
  clear desk policies, 38-9
  communication style, 66-77
  delegating, 39
  fighting fires, 35-6
  goal setting and planning, 52-3
  image, 57-65
  management-imposed activities, 34
  meetings, 39-42
  personal objectives, 77-80
  personal time profile, 44-57
  procrastination, 54-5
  staff-imposed activities, 34-5
  stress, 56-7
  time management, 32-57
  time principles, 53-4
  using lists, 36-8
personal leadership profiles, 90-106
personal time profile, 44-57
Peter principle, 186-7
phone calls, 61
physical environment, 183-5
planning:
  capacity planning, 19-23
  implementation, 25-6
  objectives, 14-27
  planning, 9, 24-5
political environment, 124-5
power, information and, 190-1
power dressing, 63
priorities, 35
private life:
  families, 42-3
  goals, 79-80
procrastination, 54-5
progress, motivation and, 177

questions, communication skills, 76

reassigning staff, 143-4
recognition, motivation and, 172, 176, 216, 219
recruitment, 141-3
Reddin, William, 123
resources:
  action plans, 25
  defining, 9, 19-23
  human, 128-52
responsibility:
  managers, 6-7
  teams, 129-34

safety and security, incentives, 173
salespeople:
  management contact, 84-5
  sales meetings, 217-21

self-actualisation, 173
self-confidence, 154
self-imposed activities, 34-5
skills:
   coaching, 159-61
   training, 145, 164-6
spoken communication, 73-7
staff, 128-52, 158, 164-6
   annual appraisals, 146-50
   characteristics profile, 134-41
   coaching, 158-64
   commitment, 199-200
   communication, 185-92
   development, 153-67
   forced ranking, 148-50
   foreign nationals, 123-6
   implementing job specifications, 146
   job profiles, 134-41
   job specification, 129-34
   manipulation, 10
   motivation, 9, 10-11, 168-70
   performance standards, 130, 131-4, 146-50
   reassigning, 143-4
   recruiting, 129, 141-3
   training, 144-5
staff characteristics profiles, 134-41
status levels, incentives, 173
straight talking, 10-11
strategy, action plans, 24
stress, 56-7
summary sheets, 189
survival, motivation, 171

tasks, achieving, 6
team meetings, 217-21
teams:
   annual appraisals, 146-50
   building, 6, 104-5
   characteristics profile, 134-41
   coaching, 158-64
   commitment, 199-200
   communication, 185-92
   development, 153-67
   forced ranking, 148-50
   foreign nationals, 123-6
   implementing job specifications, 146
   job profiles, 134-41
   job specification, 129-34
   management style, 104-5
   members, 128-52
   motivation, 168-70
   performance standards, 130, 131-4, 146-50
   reassigning, 143-4
   recruiting, 129, 141-3
   training, 144-5, 158, 164-6
technical knowledge, training, 145
time management, 32-57
   achieving objectives, 33-4
   assertiveness, 55-6
   balance, 42-3
   being organised, 32-6
   clear desk policies, 38-9
   delegating, 39
   fighting fires, 35-6
   goal setting and planning, 52-3
   management-imposed activities, 34
   meetings, 39-42
   personal time profile, 44-57
   procrastination, 54-5
   staff-imposed activities, 34-5
   stress, 56-7
   time principles, 53-4
   using lists, 36-8
trade union influence, 124
training, 144-5, 158, 164-6

group, 218
  meetings and, 40

union influences, 124
urgent matters, 35-6

verbal skills, 74-7
visitors, offices, 59-62

welcoming visitors, 61
work conditions, 9, 11-12

workaholics, 42-3
working environment, 9, 59-62, 183-93
  accessibility, 62
  communication, 185-92
  layout, 59-60
  location, 58
  physical environment, 183-5
  psychological environment, 185-92
  visitors, 61

About the Author:

Alasdair White is a consultant specialising in human resource management and organisational development. Working for Performance Management Solutions Ltd, he is based near Brussels, where he has an international practice, covering Europe, the Middle East and the Far East. Clients include international banks such as Citibank and Standard Chartered Bank, insurance companies, multi-nationals like IBM, and the European Commission. He is an active member of the Institute of Directors and is a visiting lecturer at the London Management Centre at the University of Westminster. He is the author of CONTINUOUS QUALITY IMPROVEMENT: A HANDS-ON GUIDE TO SETTING UP AND SUSTAINING A COST-EFFECTIVE QUALITY PROGRAMME.